Twice Burned

Paul A. Samakow, Esq.

*Member, American Association of Justice,
Burn Injury Litigation Group

*Member, American Burn Association

Acknowledgements

I want to thank Vania Yanez for her extensive assistance in research and "fact-checking" that allowed me to put this book together.

I also want to thank my editor Dave Vasudevan for his skill in assembling my content and putting it together into this book's format.

Finally I want to thank my wife, Susan, for her continuing support and encouragement with all of my work, and her always valuable and needed common sense perspective on everything I do.

Contents

Introduction

Please do not be "burned twice."

Investigate the potential for obtaining compensation after you have suffered a burn injury. If you do not do this, if you do not investigate, if you do not at least talk to a lawyer (we do not charge for consultations), you truly will be "burned" twice.

Burn survivors are resilient. Strong. Unfortunately, too often, they are unaware that there may be significant compensation available to them, to address the torment they have endured and will endure. Others who caused that torment can be legally required to pay.

This book is being written for burn survivors and their families—the caregivers—to educate, provide information about legal rights and the potential for compensation, and to provide resources. Survivors are among society's strongest people; their caregivers are true heroes. Both need the information in this book.

Individuals who are involved in automobile collisions quickly come to ask who will pay for their medical treatment, who will reimburse the money they lose because they miss work, and who will compensate them for the pain and suffering.

Far too many burn survivors do not ask questions about compensation. One of the reasons, perhaps the primary reason, is that survivors, and their families are consumed with survival, medical treatment, and simply just getting better.

Here, you will learn the answers to those compensation questions.

Here, also, I have provided excellent resources for survivors and caregivers.

When I was eight years old, our next-door neighbors' house burned down. My parents took them in. One night I overheard (the classic scene of the child on the stairwell listening to the adults talking) that our neighbors' insurance company was not paying for anything—money these people needed and deserved. There was talk about getting a lawyer. My career was cemented. Even at that early age I knew that what was happening was wrong. I knew then that I wanted to be someone who helped people who needed and deserved money, to right wrongs done by others. To right wrongs done by insurance companies. Little did I know then how outrageous the insurance industry's conduct truly was. For my entire career as an attorney I have seen, and fought, insurance injustice.

1

This memory—of good people crying at my kitchen table—was awakened after I was hired to represent a little boy who was horribly scalded by scalding hot bathtub water. Memories came back of the fire. Memories came back of a bad insurance company. The little boy underwent more surgical procedures by the time he was two than anybody should ever have to endure. Then, more excruciatingly painful surgeries to remove scars that don't grow when the skin does, debridement procedures, grafts, and therapy, until he stops growing. He wears pressure garments. As he gets older, and in school, he will suffer bullying, stares, unkind words. Hopefully, he will not suffer loss of self-esteem or confidence.

My mission was clear. My heart was been totally taken by this little boy. The insurance companies don't care that their insured created a disaster waiting to happen. I know this because I've been dealing with insurance companies for over four decades, and they very rarely, if ever, do what they should. They fight. They delay, stall and try to avoid providing needed and deserved compensation.

My life's mission is and has been since meeting this little boy, to help burn survivors.

When I took on this little boy's case, I educated myself by reading, learning, watching videos for days, talking to anyone who might share knowledge with me, and by reaching out to numerous and top experts in fields of engineering, science, medicine, psychology, and more. Within the United States there are people, angels, whose lives are dedicated to helping burn survivors. I have found them, and they now know me. I am proud to say I am now one of them, the "burn community." I will bring my knowledge and that of these angels' collectively to my client's case. And to any and all cases I might be fortunate enough (and honored) to take on in the future.

Burn injuries, mostly, do not have to happen. They do, unfortunately, more often than most of us understand. When a water heater doesn't have safety mechanisms, when a fire starts because of faulty equipment, when an apparatus explodes, when chemicals or radiation leaks, more often than not it is because of negligence. When a child's pajamas catch fire and explode it is because the clothing manufacturer failed to construct them properly. The reasons for burns are many, and too often, again, it is because someone did something wrong, or failed to do something.

The law provides compensation for individuals who suffer because of the negligence of others.

This book is dedicated to my first burn injury client, the little boy, and it is my hope that any who read this will come to learn about more about burns, about resources available, and about survivors' legal rights to compensation. I further hope that all reading this will learn from the stories that I have sprinkled in. I said above that burn survivors are among the strongest individuals in our society—I know this intuitively, because first, they survived, and second, they had to exercise their resilience muscle. I learned these amazing people are not "victims." I know they are strong, because I have read hundreds of stories, some of which I have repeated in a summary manner in this book, and I have taken great comfort in reading them and seeing how they came through their original torment. Burn survivors do not have to be shunned as "different,"— people can and do embrace them as examples of courage, resilience and strength. Burn survivors are our greatest examples of dealing with obstacles thrown at them.

Caregivers are an entirely different breed of people. They are absolutely true angels. They sacrifice, they worry, they go above and beyond, every day, almost every waking moment in the beginning, to protect and provide for their burn survivor. They too need care. They need to make sure they do not "burn out." The term used is "compassion fatigue." I will discuss and explain this in the chapter in this book devoted to caregivers.

We've all been burned.

Both figuratively and literally, of course. There is a difference between a minor kitchen "oops" that results in a putting a bandage on a finger, and a severe burn that leaves you with a permanent disability and scarring.

While some accidents that leave you with a burn injury are no one's fault (after all, some accidents are just accidents), sometimes your burn is the result of negligence for which someone should be liable.

If that is the case, there is a very real possibility that money (in many cases a significant amount of money) can be obtained through a personal injury lawsuit or workers' compensation claim.

You simply must investigate to find out.

AND YOU SHOULD MAKE IMMEDIATE NOTE—THERE IS A DEADLINE, A TIME DEADLINE, IN WHICH TO MAKE A CLAIM. IN MOST STATES IT IS EITHER 2 OR 3 YEARS. INVESTIGATE NOW. IF YOU WAIT, OR ARE TOO LATE, YOU MIGHT LOSE ALL POSSIBILITY OF RECOVERING SIGNICANT, AND MOST PROBABLY NEEDED, COMPENSATION.

Thank you for reading this. I hope it has value for you.

CHAPTER 1

The Need for Compensation—The High Cost of Caring For Burn Injuries

Unlike some injuries that require a short period of medical attention, and then that get better, burn injuries, the serious ones, often require extensive and perhaps long-term medical and other types of care. The real cost of this care can be astronomical.

> *Please note—the statistics identified in this book (current to December 2020) are from national associations and organizations, and these are identified where possible. Similarly, "costs" as identified in this book for medical care and other expenses are from numerous medical publications, websites and other sources. The costs in all cases are averages and should not be relied upon for any specific care rendered or expense incurred.*

To begin, the **American Burn Association** keeps statistics, and they reveal that, on average, each year nearly 500,000 Americans receive medical treatment for burn injuries, including 40,000 hospitalizations and more than 3,200 deaths from fire and smoke inhalation. Moreover, again, on average, someone dies from a fire or smoke inhalation every two hours and 41 minutes.

The path to recovery for burn-injuries can be long and costly. Putting the physical and psychological pain aside, the financial burden can be enormous. In the United States, burn-related medical costs (per the ABA) exceed $1.5 billion per year, and indirect costs exceed $5 billion per year. The average cost of a burn-related hospital stay is $24,000, more than double the cost of non-burn related stays. Paradigm Outcomes, a case management company, estimated that in complicated cases severe burns can cost up to **$10 million** to be completely treated.

Why are burn injuries so expensive to treat?

Moderate to severe burns can damage many systems in the body, creating varied and multiple medical problems. This is what makes them so expensive to treat. Some of the injuries that result from burns include:

- Damage to the outer layer (epidermis) of the skin.
- Nerve damage of the body if the burn disrupts or damages the neuropathic system
- Bacterial infection, which may lead to a bloodstream infection (sepsis)
- Fluid loss, including low blood volume (hypovolemia)
- Dangerously low body temperature (hypothermia)
- Muscle, ligament, and tendon damage
- Breathing problems from the intake of hot air or smoke
- Scars or ridged areas caused by an overgrowth of scar tissue (keloids)
- Bone and joint problems, such as when scar tissue causes the shortening and tightening of skin, muscles or tendons (contractures)
- Contracture (shortening or stiffening of connective tissue)
- Eye/vision damage

A quick understanding of the potential damage to skin is in order. Normal skin consists of two main layers: the outer layer, or epidermis, and the layer "below" the epidermis, called the dermis. The outer layer acts as the first line of defense to the environment. The inner layer contains glands, hair follicle roots and capillaries. When a burn occurs, the skin is compromised and its "barrier" is, as well. This means that very specific functions can be adversely affected:

- Protection against infection
- Protection against body fluid loss, which would normally prevent dehydration
- Controlling of body temperature
- Excretion of some waste products
- Reduced reception of sensory stimuli
- Reduced production of vitamin D

These essential functions are reduced with a partial thickness burn and they are completely eliminated with a full thickness burn.

When injuries are severe, life altering, or catastrophic, they will likely require many medical and mental-health professionals to treat the survivor to help with the various phases of care. Here are the recognized "phases" of this care:

- Phase One—Emergent Care: Surgeons will be involved in this "immediate" care, and the main focus is on stopping and accessing the burn and keeping vital organs functioning. This phase is typically the first few days post-burn. The severity of the burn is determined, and urgent care is provided. Vital signs remain monitored and all fluids taken in and eliminated are recorded. Observation is ongoing for signs of potential complications. Stabilization occurs and includes addressing airway and breathing issues, and hydration issues. Burns cause fluid loss and often, intravenous lines are inserted to assure that hydration is ongoing. A feeding tube may be used if needed. Initial debridement and dressing takes place once the wounds are stabilized and cleaned.

- Phase Two—Acute Care: Pain management and wound care specialists will then focus on preventing infection and promoting the healing process. This phase begins and remains until all full-thickness wounds are covered by skin grafts. The objectives during this phase include removal of dead tissue and covering the wounds with skin grafts, providing adequate nutrition and hydration, preventing complications and contractures, and meeting with the survivor and his or her family to address **both** of their evolving physical and emotional needs.

- Phase Three—Rehabilitative Care: Occupational, psychological and physical therapists and reconstructive surgeons will be involved with the long-term care—improving mobility, relieving pain, reducing the appearance of scars, providing emotional support and finding financial support. Plastic surgeons may continue to be involved, particularly for children, to revise scars, because as the child ages and grows, the scars do not expand and grow, so those scars have to be removed, or excised. For children this can mean repeated surgeries, until the child stops growing.

Other continuing expenses can include daily medications like painkillers and antibiotics, blood transfusions, wound dressings, and pressure bandages. Additionally, if a survivor needs to return to a burn treatment center or hospital for continuing procedures, expenses can add dramatically.

Continuing, there are three common surgeries that burn survivors might undergo (depending on the severity of the burn):

- **Debridement** is a procedure for treating a wound in the skin. It involves thoroughly cleaning the wound and removing all hyperkeratotic (thickened skin or callus), infected, and nonviable (necrotic or dead) tissue, foreign debris, and residual material from dressings. Burn debridement can be done by several different methods. They include surgical, chemical, mechanical, or autolytic tissue removal. Debridement may need to be done multiple times as the burned area heals. On average, debridement costs $500 per procedure. This is primarily a surgeon's fee, and does not include anesthesia or facility charges, as these can vary widely by facility and location.

- **Dermabrasion** is a surgical procedure involving the removal (sanding) of the damaged top layer of the skin using a specialized instrument called a dermabrader. Dermabrasion improves the appearance of the scar or other skin abnormality as a new layer of skin will replace the skin that has been treated. This procedure won't entirely remove the scar, but it will improve its appearance by softening the edges of the scar or other lesions. The average cost of dermabrasion is $1,296, according to 2019 statistics from the American Society of Plastic Surgeons. This average cost is only part of the total price—again, as above for debridement, it does not include anesthesia, operating room facilities or other related expenses.

- **Skin grafting** involves taking healthy skin from one part of the body and attaching, or grafting, it to an area where the skin has been damaged either because of a burn or on account of some other injury. The deeper the wound, the more tissue must be extracted from an area of the body with healthy skin.

Skin graft surgery can be quite painful, and it will usually involve anesthesia and a hospital stay of a few days. Further, even after a skin graft, the area around a burn will not look the same as uninjured skin. More upsetting, after a skin graft, a person will have two wounds, the original area of the burn and the area from which the doctor extracted skin. On average, a skin graft will cost about $18,000. However, the procedure can cost as much as about $28,000. Hopefully, a survivor will have quality health insurance, but many people who do not will have to bear these expenses on their own.

*Understanding the enormity of the real and actual costs of burn care is why it is so important to understand one's rights.

More Compensation Needed: Psychological Distress after a Burn Injury

Most people experience some degree of psychological distress after a burn injury, some more so than others. Of greatest concern is the psychological trauma children suffer. Burn survivors may have symptoms of depression, anxiety, post-traumatic stress disorder (PTSD), and body image concerns—all of which can make it difficult to transition back into normal life. Fortunately, there are numerous therapies, both medical and non-medical, that target some of these psychological and emotional issues burn survivors face and that can help them regain a sense of wellbeing.

Again, particularly for children, the stress that can accompany burn injuries can be increased in school settings, where simple stares from other children or bullying comments can compound an already fragile situation.

Body Image

Because burns can affect the way survivors' bodies function and look, the injury can greatly damage a survivor's sense of self. Many burn survivors have to deal with body image distress, a major, difficult-to-overcome psychological issue. In fact, over one-third of burn survivors report significant distress about body function and body image after a burn injury.

It is impossible to tell how a change in appearance will affect a burn survivor. Depending upon the patient, the change in their appearance can vary as to how it affects them. Of note is that the size of the wounds and scars are not necessarily a good indicator of how much distress someone will experience. A small burn scar may traumatize one burn survivor, while another might be relatively unfazed by large scars.

Burn patients with large burns, full-thickness burns, or burns on the face are generally more susceptible to appearance-related psychological issues. Poor body image is often associated with feeling ugly and unattractive, worrying about how a partner may react to scars, problems with sexuality and intimate settings, rejection, social discomfort and anxiety, depression and post-traumatic stress disorder.

Intimacy

Severe burns often leave behind scarring, changing how the survivor's body looks as well as how it works. Some people worry about their partners seeing their burn scars during intimate moments, while others struggle to adapt to life with limited mobility or functioning. It is important to remember that this is absolutely normal for burn survivors and intimacy after a burn injury is possible.

How do burns and burn treatment affect intimacy?

- Physical impairment, including amputations or limited mobility
- Extreme fatigue
- Diminished sex drive from medications
- Intense itching
- Chronic pain
- Increased sensitivity
- Lack of sensation
- Depression or anxiety
- Altered body image
- Skin integrity issues

Psychologists and burn injury therapists are correct, and quick to point out that both participants in intimate relationships should remember that intimacy is about far more than sexual activity. Many couples are able to rekindle their intimacy by focusing on being romantic with one another in other, less physical ways. This includes affection such as kissing, hand-holding and cuddling, spending time together in intimate settings, and even just taking the time to talk to one another with no distractions.

More potential expense—complications

Unfortunately, complications from burn injuries happen more often than not.

When a patient is dealing with serious burns and complications arise, expenses can add up very quickly. Common complications and their general costs are:

- Scarring, disfigurement, and contracture, which could mean an additional $35,000 in costs or more. Around two-thirds of people hospitalized with burn injuries experience one or more of these complications.
- Psychological difficulties arising from burns, which can reach or exceed $75,000, or even more, with continuing need for treatment. Approximately 57 percent of survivors suffer from psychological problems, including post-traumatic stress disorder (PTSD), after a moderate to serious burn.

- Skin breakdown, or "fragile skin," can add over $100,000 to treatment costs. Skin breakdown occurs in 55 percent of cases.

- Infections of all types—cellulitis, septicemia, pneumonia, and others—can add $120,000 to costs. Over one-third (35 percent) of hospitalized burn survivors experience one or more infections, and sometimes organ failure due to the infections.

- Skin graft failure or wounds that are slow to heal happen almost one-third (32 percent) of the time and can translate into an additional $110,000 in costs.

Medical costs also increase when the burn injury affects the breathing system (inhalation), if there is a corneal (eye) injury, or if the burn has created chronic pain.

Non-medical costs can be substantial

After the burn survivor goes home from the initial hospital stay, the family vehicle or the home may require costly modifications. Additionally, medical equipment such as walkers or wheelchairs, orthotics, and prosthetics, along with home health care, can cause mounting bills.

Further, unfortunately, the costs may not necessarily end there. If the burn survivor has a lengthy period of being disabled, or is permanently disabled, lost income can be a significant problem; benefits, wages, bonuses, and commissions may be included. Lost wages and benefits can easily reach into the seven figures, depending on the burn survivor's age and circumstances. When the family breadwinner can no longer do his or her job, everyone suffers financially.

Burns can happen to anyone—children, spouses, parents, and siblings. When a burn is serious the costs must be measured both in dollars and in emotional trauma.

When a burn is due to someone else's negligence, they should be the one to shoulder the financial costs that the survivor and their family undergo. Understand that burn injury "costs" are not limited to monetary ones, and the negligent party must be responsible for these as well.

In summary, determining what an "appropriate" amount of compensation might be will not happen quickly. When someone suffers a burn injury, the full extent of that injury, and all of the consequences will most probably take a long time to appreciate.

Survivors may want to take an early settlement from an insurance company in order to move on and start paying bills. However, as is often the case, these settlements may not reflect the full and fair compensation you need.

Before agreeing to a low settlement after a burn injury, please read this book and learn what you should know going forward. You can take the right first step by hiring an attorney.

Burn Injury Claims—How They Usually Works

After a burn injury, the insurance company may contact you by offering a preliminary settlement. This contact is made because the insurance company wants to push the claim through quickly in the hopes you will take what they offer and not file a lawsuit. They know that once you hire a lawyer, their chances drastically decrease in terms of getting you to agree to a lowball offer. Taking this initial settlement offer without speaking to a burn injury lawyer could mean you won't get the compensation necessary to adequately handle your losses from the injury.

Not all burns warrant a legal fight, mind you.

If you have suffered a serious burn, you should always err on the side of caution and discuss your claim with an attorney. Attorneys will always discuss your case with you at no cost, so you have nothing to lose by making the telephone call. Severe burns mean you will likely have to go through a complex rehabilitation process that could take multiple surgeries and therapy sessions over many months or years to address. Even your treating physician may not realize the full extent of your injuries and the treatment required until they get the results of initial therapies. This all takes time. It's wise to wait. Your future, and in all probability, money you will need cannot be determined quickly, just because an insurance company is at the door with a few dollars. You should wait until you have as much information as possible.

Choosing the Right Burn Injury Attorney

This is where the right attorney comes in. The one you select will work to get you settlement terms that are fair and more in line with your injuries. Most personal injury cases take place outside the courtroom. From research to discovery to negotiations, many steps have to be taken before a case goes to trial. Don't be concerned now. The truth is that most cases don't go to court. This is a testament to the skill of your lawyers as they try everything in their power to get the insurance company to pay up.

*Please also refer to the Conclusion of this book on choosing the right attorney to represent you.

CHAPTER **2**

The Need for an Attorney and Components of Your Compensation Claim

The survivor of a burn injury enters a complicated new world of physical, emotional, psychological and social distress. These concerns are challenging. Beyond doctors and counsellors, seeking legal help during the early stages of recovery helps minimize financial and psychological pressure on both the survivor and his or her family.

It is impossible to properly fully diagnose yourself and give yourself medical care for burn injuries. It is similarly impossible for a burn survivor to conduct all of the crucial legal matters in an effort to obtain compensation. Imagine a severe burn survivor, in the months following the burn, trying to investigate liability, preserve evidence, gather information, interview witnesses, determine who is responsible, arrange for expert witnesses, and more. Impossible. Further, knowing how to navigate all of this in the proper way within the requirements of the legal system is still even more impossible.

The claims of a burn survivor are not those taken up in small claims court. It is, without question, imperative that you hire an attorney to assure that you have the opportunity to obtain full compensation.

When should you consult an attorney?

Very simply, you should consult an attorney as soon as possible. The sooner, the better, to allow the attorney to begin an investigation, contact witnesses, and to assure that evidence is not lost or destroyed.

Every state has a law called The Statute of Limitations. This is a "deadline" law—a time limit in which someone injured must act—either "settle" the case or file a lawsuit. Many states have a two-year deadline. Some have three-year deadlines. This means the case must be settled, or a lawsuit must be filed timely, or no claim can be made.

A) Legal Rights of Burn Survivors—the Basics

Of immediate and particular concern to the burn survivor is how to pay for everything, or moreover, anything in the aftermath of a burn injury. Financial worries arise from the myriad of questions and scenarios immediately confronting the survivor and their family. How will mounting medical bills be paid, both past and future? How can living expenses be paid while the survivor is unable to work? Who will take care of the patient? What will be the long-term impact on finances? Burn injuries require treatments that take a lot of time, and rehabilitation of the patient is expensive, which adds to the overwhelming debt-burden of the burn survivor.

As discussed in Chapter One, burn injury survivors are often plagued by a painful injury, disfigurement, organ damage, marked sensitivity to temperature change, damage to body chemistry, and emotional and physical trauma. Yet despite the severity of these health issues, survivors are often unaware of the benefits about seeking legal help. Often the survivor fears the cost of legal intervention.

So, to be 100% clear: It costs the survivor NOTHING to talk to an attorney, and it costs NOTHING to hire an attorney.

Attorneys take these cases on what is referred to as a "contingent" basis. This means they do not charge up front, they do not ask for a retainer, they do not charge hourly or bill their clients, but rather, they take a percentage of the recovery—AT THE END OF THE LEGAL CASE—before they get paid. The "contingent" part is that their fee, the payment for their work, relies on their ability to recover compensation for their client. If there is no recovery, the attorney receives no payment, at all. Nothing.

Clients quickly understand that the attorney will work very hard, because if they don't do good work, they get nothing.

To repeat: There is no financial risk in consulting a qualified attorney about the details of a burn injury case.

Another reason individuals may not look for legal help is that they believe the accident or injury was in some way caused by them. This may not be the case, but, even if the injured individual is partially at fault, recovering a substantial monetary is still very possible.

B) What are Claims Based On?

Several legal theories can present for claims for compensation:

- Recklessness—example: a vehicle explosion following an automobile collision, where the at-fault party was traveling at an excessively high rate of speed

- Negligence—example: a maintenance worker fails to properly repair equipment

- Intentional act—If someone intentionally acted in a way that caused your injuries, whether that someone is the owner of a property where you were burned or if they were an employee, then you can file a lawsuit directly against the owner and/or the employee who harmed you. <u>However, of significant note: intentional acts are normally excluded from insurance coverage</u>.

- Product failure or partial failure (called product liability), or failure to warn

- Faulty equipment—example: toaster oven, air-fryer, microwave explosion

A frequently asked question in the aftermath of a burn injury is what amount of compensation a burn survivor is entitled to receive. There is no immediate or even short-term monetary answer to this question, because there are many types of damages that a burn injury survivor may obtain—and many variables that determine them. I tell clients it is like a baseball game. You cannot predict the outcome of the game in the first inning. We must wait until we know all of the facts, develop all of the legal theories, determine the identity of all of the potential "at-fault" parties, and lastly, but most importantly, learn the full extent and nature of the injuries.

For purposes of discussion, "damages" is the legal term for monetary compensation that is claimed by the survivor of an injury. Broadly speaking, there are two types of damages: special and general. Both of these types of damages are designed to address the survivor and the pain that he is suffering because of an accident or injury. The main purpose of these damages is to compensate the survivor for injuries sustained in an attempt to restore him to the same situation he was in prior to the injury, or, to a status as good as possible.

C) Component Parts—Legal Rights

Burn survivors need to know their legal rights, and they must understand that protecting those rights are realistically only going to be happen with the help of a lawyer. Civil law exists to compensate an individual for injuries and losses caused by a defective product, someone's negligence, or some other form of misconduct or failure to act. Legal rights to compensation include:

Payment of Past and Future Medical Bills—You may be entitled to have your medical expenses, past and future paid for, including hospitalization, surgical procedures, ongoing medical care, counseling, scar revision/ cosmetic surgery, physical therapy and occupational therapy and psychological counselling.

Compensation for Loss of Income—You may be entitled to have your lost wages, both past and future, paid.

Vocational Rehabilitation (Job Training)—You may be entitled to compensation for retraining for a new job or occupation if you can no longer perform your prior position.

Compensation for Pain and Suffering—You may be entitled to compensation for pain and suffering you have endured and may continue to endure because of your injury. This includes any number of "negative" issues, including physical, psychological, emotional pain and suffering, both past, current and future, stress, disruption of your life, aggravation, inconvenience, embarrassment, loss of some confidence and self-esteem, and much more.

Loss of Consortium—The spouse of a burn survivor may be entitled to compensation when an injury is so severe that it interferes with the injured party's spousal relations.

Wrongful Death—In a wrongful death suit, the amount of money that a survivor's family receives can be calculated based on the economic loss to the heirs, including all of the decedent's medical bills incurred by the survivor while he or she was still alive. In some states, claims for compensation for the suffering of the family whose relative died can be made.

These monetary amounts are typically determined with the assistance of medical experts, life-care planners and economists.

D) Monetary Recovery

1. **"Special" or "Economic" Damages.**

   This category of compensation is measurable. It includes medical bills and lost income, both past, ongoing, and future. It is relatively simple to calculate these damages, as it only requires looking at medical bills received and adding them. Future medical bills can be estimated and are recoverable. Regarding lost income, again, the analysis only requires calculations of salary (hourly, annual, average commission, etc.) and determining the time lost.

   Economic damages are a specific dollar amount.

2. **"General" or "Non-Economic" Damages.**

   These damages are cannot be "calculated" and are less easily measured. How much is pain worth?

The most common type of general damages is compensation for pain and suffering, as described and detailed above. Compensation for pain and suffering is over and above any monetary compensation for economic losses as just described.

When awarding general damages, a judge or jury will consider everything that is negative about the survivor's ordeal: emotional, psychological, stress, mental trauma, embarrassment, humiliation, loss of enjoyment, disruption of life, negative affect on relationships, and anything and everything else that can be attributed to the trauma that in any way adversely affected the survivor in his or her life. General damages include all of this: past, present and future.

General damage can further include recognition of an injury's effect on the survivor's family. "Loss of consortium" (loss of relations with your partner) damages are awarded to compensate a spouse for loss of emotional support and intimate relations as a direct result of the survivor's injuries.

A wrongful death suit may also result in general damages awarded to the deceased burn survivor's heirs in recognition of pain and suffering that the death has caused. Thus, wrongful death damages can be either, or both, general or specific depending on whether claimed to compensate the heirs for costs that can be measured and that are associated with the survivor's accident, or for general pain and suffering.

3. **"Putting It All Together"—Life Care Planner**

Because treatment for injuries may exceed the time limits for making a claim (called the Statute of Limitations), costs for future medical and other treatment must be considered in order to make a "complete" claim before that time limit is up. Attorneys typically employ the services of experts called Life Care Planners, who do complete and thorough investigations. These professionals typically begin by reviewing medical records, and the talking to doctors. They will next review employment records, and ultimately they can provide a report detailing the needed amount of money for an injured person for the anticipated remainder of their life.

Doctors will provide details of the care needed in the future. Work records will provide a view of what the injured person was making and allow for calculations for missed future.

If a survivor's injuries prevent him from performing a prior job, life care planners will include in their plan work-retraining costs, or costs for new education.

Life care plans for children who have permanent burn and scar injuries can reach millions of dollars, sometimes exceeding ten million dollars. For an adult, the plan, depending upon the extent of the injuries, can also reach into the millions of dollars.

4. **Punitive damages.**

In addition to the first two categories above, all called "compensatory" damages, punitive damages may be available in certain cases. Where available, these damages can be awarded and to punish for the wrongdoer's actions that caused an injury, and to hopefully stop them from happening in the future.

Punitive damages may be available in cases where someone's actions are particularly reckless. Further, punitive damages may be available where there is evidence of malice or intent. Punitive damages are "extra," in addition to compensatory damages. The awarded dollar amount of punitive damages will often be based on the egregiousness of the defendant's actions.

Avoiding Reduction of Damages

In order to ensure eligibility for full damages, a burn survivor must minimize the effects of the accident through seeking proper treatment. This is called "mitigation of damages." This means the injured person has the obligation of an injured person to act in a reasonable manner that avoids the worsening of the injury. For example, if a patient refuses to undergo treatment when a doctor recommends it to improve his condition, this patient has failed to mitigate the harmful effects of the injury. If the survivor refuses to undergo treatment recommended by a doctor to improve his condition, he may not be able to recover more money to pay for future treatments.

Severe burn injuries may present as life and death situations with crippling pain and disfigurement. Some survivors may be inclined to deny treatment. I make no comment about what any person should or should not do. Nonetheless, to maximize a damages award, it is essential that burn survivors follow their doctors' recommendations or seek additional medical opinions if they disagree with the doctor's course of treatment.

If the opposing lawyer discovers that the burn survivor failed to follow a doctor's instructions, he or she will have legal justification to argue for reduced damages. Using alternative and unproven treatments may also reduce the dollar amount of damages that a survivor can seek.

Not all mitigation of damages involves medical treatment. If a burn survivor is physically well enough to return to work and does not seek employment, he may be ineligible to continue receiving benefits. Moreover, if a successful argument is made that he is "malingering," meaning faking physical symptoms to avoid work, a decrease in compensation is very possible.

Burn survivors may endure unimaginable physical and emotional trauma with long-term consequences. It is vital for the injured person to know that civil law exists to compensate an individual for injuries and losses. The amount of that compensation can be determined in part by the injured person's actions.

What if the Burn Survivor was Partially Responsible for His or Her Injuries?

Four states and Washington, D.C. have a law called "contributory negligence." This is a very harsh law and it bars someone from recovering, even if the injured person is found to be one percent responsible for their own injury. The finding of any contribution will literally prohibit recovery. The four states are Virginia, Maryland, Alabama and North Carolina.

All of the other states have a law called "comparative negligence."

While the specifics of laws vary from state to state, generally, the law means that a burn survivor can recover as long as his or her contribution to the underlying event was less than fifty percent. Then, if contribution is found, the recovery will be reduced by the percentage that the survivor contributed to their injury.

An example, in simple terms: If a survivor contributed 10% to his or her injury, and a verdict is recovered in the amount $1000, the survivor would then recover $900, as the survivor's ten percent contribution would be used to reduce the monetary award by that percentage.

E) Burn injuries—Who Should Be Held Liable?

The potential "responsible" parties are many, and in any given case may be many, depending upon circumstances. Here is a partial list of those who can be accountable for burn injuries:

- The owner or driver, or both, of a vehicle that causes a crash resulting in a fire;

- Landlords
- The manufacturer of a product
- A gas company that causes an explosion
- A water heater manufacturer
- A plumber
- A propane company
- A maintenance company
- An electrician

A burn injury can be serious. If you've been burned and you believe you are not at fault, you should immediately contact an attorney so that he or she can help you through the process of filing a lawsuit. You may be entitled to (and you would clearly deserve) compensation.

More Examples—It requires an attorney to fully investigate these and it almost always requires the involvement of expert witnesses to determine fault and testify in court if necessary, to prove fault.

Numerous parties may have responsibility, alone or with others, for burn injuries:

Defective Smoke Alarm

Injuries can include severe burns, smoke inhalation, kidney failure, and amputation. Landlords, building owners, maintenance companies, and manufacturers may be responsible.

Chemical Burns

Chemical burns can be caused by acids, bases, and hydrocarbons. The severity depends on the concentration of the substance, the length of exposure, and the type of chemical causing the damage. Lack of warning notices can lead to responsibility.

Electrical Burns

When electricity passes through a resistant material such as the human body, energy (basically) turns into heat. The extent of the injury depends on the size of the current, the pathway (head to toe, hand to hand, etc.), and the length of exposure. Malfunctions, lack of maintenance, lack of warnings can lead to responsibility for employers, building owners and others.

CO Poisoning Inhalation

The most common source of fire-caused inhalation injuries caused by an asphyxiant are those caused by carbon monoxide. Carbon monoxide (CO) is released during the burning of all organic materials. Landlords, building owners, employers and maintenance companies may be responsible to compensate a survivor.

Chemical Inhalation Injuries

Chemical inhalation injuries are highly varied and completely dependent on the toxin causing the injury, the concentration inhaled, and the length of exposure. The size of the particles inhaled also affects the type of injury. Larger particles remain in the nasopharynx and major airways. Small particles that can diffuse easily can move into smaller airways and alveoli, potentially causing more severe damage than larger particles. Landlords, building owners, employers and maintenance companies may be responsible.

Inhalation Injury and Respiratory Failure

Inhalation injury occurs in between 2.5% and 15% of victims. It can even be present if no burn has occurred, merely through exposure to inhalants. Landlords, building owners, employers and maintenance companies may be responsible.

Scald Injury

Children are particularly at risk for these. It only takes a few seconds to be severely injured. Landlords, building owners, water-heater manufacturers, and maintenance companies are among some that may be responsible.

Natural Gas Explosion

Horrible pain and disfigurement can result from gas explosion injuries. A city entity or a county, or a gas company, an employer, or an owner of property are among some who may be responsible.

F) How Long Will It Take, and What is the Legal Process to Recover Compensation?

Aside from knowing what they can recover, most survivors that have suffered burn injuries like to know how long it will take them to recover compensation. This is a complicated question. The timeline for any given case will largely be determined by the choices the survivor makes, as well as the length of his or her recovery for the injuries. The first and most important factor is always how the survivor is progressing with his or her injury from a medical standpoint. Trying to resolve a case early on might deprive a survivor of including both special and general damages compensation, such as medical bills for services not yet provided, lost wages for future work, and compensation for psychological damages that might not be fully appreciated at an early stage.

Settling a claim—before even filing a lawsuit—can take a full year, or longer. If there is a decision to pursue certain kinds of damages, it can lengthen the time because that will involve finding and preparing both lay and expert witnesses and preparing for trial.

Burn injury cases usually take between one and two years to resolve because of their general complexity. These are not simple "rear-end" automobile accident claims.

If a settlement cannot be reached a burn injury lawyer will file a lawsuit and prepare to take the case to trial. A pre-trial settlement is always possible. Often courts require a mediation hearing, and sometimes an arbitration process. Either can get the case resolved.

A mediation hearing is much less formal than a trial. The mediation process is much faster than going to court, and it is much less expensive. The process essentially involves a neutral mediator who is selected by the parties, and who then attempts to resolve the case for the parties. The attorneys and the parties participate in the process but in a much less formal way than "testifying" in a courtroom. These hearings often result in resolving the case, as neither side typically wants to take the risk of going to court, and neither wants to incur the expense of doing so. Nonetheless, mediation is not a guarantee the case will be resolved.

An arbitration hearing is also a less formal process than going to court. It too is less expensive and faster. In arbitration, the Arbitrator decides the result. The Arbitrator is also someone selected by the parties, and again, both the attorneys and the parties participate.

If a lawsuit is filed, the typical steps the attorney for the survivor will take are as follows:

- Filing the lawsuit
- Conducting discovery to recover relevant information and evidence

Discovery involves preparing written questions called interrogatories for the other party to answer, taking depositions of all individuals with knowledge of anything related to the case, to preserve testimony and evidence, requesting documents and other physical evidence (videos for example), and asking for "admissions" by the other party

- Filing and arguing motions in advance of trial
- Conducting the trial before a judge or jury

These lawsuits, as seen, can require expert testimony to prove fault, to prove exactly what occurred, and to explain injuries. Although it may all seem obvious, the law requires these experts to provide their opinions.

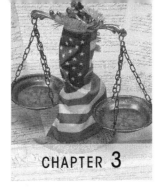

CHAPTER 3

Where Burn Injuries Can Occur

A burn injury can occur anywhere. Even one percent more vigilance than might ordinarily be the case in your daily routine can prevent irreparable harm.

Who is At Risk?

Despite the commonly understood concept that men are daredevils, women have slightly higher rates of death from burns compared to males according to the most recent data.

The higher risk for females is associated with burn injuries occurring in the home, with open fire cooking, or inherently unsafe cookstoves, which can ignite loose clothing. Open flames used for heating, and lightning also pose risks.

Along with adult women, children are particularly vulnerable to burns. Children's burns and scalds typically happen by contact with hot food or water. These pediatric scalding burns occur 200,000 times per year (American Burn Association). Each year, 250,000 children require treatment for burn injuries, 15,000 children need hospitalization and 1,100 die.

Every day, over 300 children infants to those up to age 19 are treated in emergency rooms for burn-related injuries and two children die because of being burned. Younger children are more likely to sustain injuries from scald burns caused by hot liquids or steam, while older children are more likely to sustain injuries from flame burns caused by direct contact with fire.

Where Most Burn Injuries Occur

A) Your Home / Your Apartment

Over 73% of burn injuries and deaths occur at home. House fires are one of the most common causes of burn injury that result in death.

According to the National Fire Protection Association (NFPA), fire departments responded to approximately 1,291,500 house fires in 2019. As many as 3,700 civilians died and 16,600 were injured.

The top causes of house fires include cooking mishaps, faulty or improperly usage of heating equipment, electrical hazards, smoking indoors, and knocked over or forgotten candles.

Children and women are more often burned in their homes, and most often it is in their kitchens.

Residential fires can be caused by:

- Faulty wiring
- Malfunctioning smoke detectors
- Defective appliances, such as space heaters
- A contractor who took shortcuts
- A propane appliance or supplier
- Negligent repairmen

Any number of things can cause a home fire, some of which are attributable to the negligence of others. Examples can include errors by technicians, plumbers, heating or cooling system malfunctions that can relate to product design or installation or maintenance, and much more. Again, in the event of a home fire, there is absolutely no reason not to consult an attorney to inquire about potential compensation if someone in the home is injured.

The **National Fire Incident Reporting System** is the nation's largest database of fire incident information.

From the National Fire Incident Reporting System website:

Importance of Smoke Detectors

People die in home fires. Many of these people die in homes that do not have working smoke alarms. Smoke alarms warn you and your family when there is a fire. Smoke is a deadly mix of particles and gas that is created when materials are on fire. Smoke alarms warn you there is a fire before you see, hear or smell it. Smoke alarms give you extra time to escape. Put working smoke alarms on every level of your home, inside bedrooms and outside sleeping areas. For the best protection, have interconnected smoke alarms. If one alarm sounds, they all sound. Test your smoke alarms to make sure everyone in the home can hear them, even when they are asleep. Test each alarm every month using the test button. Dust or vacuum your smoke alarms each year when you change the battery.

Cigarette Smoking Danger

Smoking is the leading cause of home fire deaths for adults 65 and over. It is also the third leading cause of fire injuries for older adults. If you smoke, smoke outside. Use deep, sturdy ashtrays. Make sure cigarette butts and ashes are completely cool before throwing them out. Check furniture and places where people smoke before you leave your home or go to bed. Keep smoking materials, including lighters and cigarettes, up high and out of the reach of children. Use child-safety locks where you store your smoking materials.

Danger in the Kitchen

Cooking fires are the number one cause of home fires. Many older adults experience burn-related injuries during cooking. Prevent fires and burns by being watchful and alert when you cook. Stay in the kitchen when you are frying, grilling, boiling or broiling food. If you leave the kitchen, even briefly, turn off the stove. If you are simmering, baking, or roasting food, check it regularly. Remain in the home while food is cooking, and use a timer to remind yourself that you are cooking. Keep a pot lid nearby when you cook. If a fire starts in the pan, you can slide the lid over the pot and turn off the burner. Clean your oven and stove top after each use. Keep anything that can burn away from the stovetop.

Wiring in Older Homes

Older homes are more likely to catch fire from electrical causes than newer homes. Wiring in these homes may not have the capacity to handle newer appliances and equipment, and these homes may not have updated safety features. Have a licensed electrician check your electrical system if you have frequent blown fuses or tripped circuit breakers. Do not overload electrical circuits. Tripping breakers or fuses usually means the circuit is overloaded.

Fire Chief Interviews

After some stellar conversations with several Fire Chiefs in major U.S. cities, I want to share their observations.

The number one thing people can do to save lives is to assure their home has working smoke detectors. One Chief I talked to in Virginia indicated that the smoke detector is an essential alarm—simply put: when alarms are working (check the batteries) they save lives. He told me that a working smoke detector more than doubles someone's chances of getting out of their home alive. He further commented that this time is critical because fires burn both hotter and faster in today's homes than twenty years ago, due to the fabrics, primarily synthetics that are in many items in the home, such as furniture. **I learned that fires double in size in less than one minute,** so again, having that detector or alarm is of the highest importance.

My Virginia Fire Chief added that where homes use gas devices (cooking), carbon monoxide detectors are very important. Gas certainly can kill.

Next, the Chiefs all agreed that it is vital to have a plan for exiting the home in the event of a fire, and a place to meet. They all said that this applies more when there are children in the home.

The Chiefs also all agreed that the number one cause of fires in homes is unattended kitchen cooking. The next leading cause of home fires, interestingly, is improperly discarded smoking materials, both legal and illegal, like marijuana (in some places still illegal), cigarettes and cigars. Third are fireplace ashes that were not disposed of properly.

Other causes of home fires are unattended candles, and improper storage of space heaters.

Electricity Burns

Many individuals suffer electricity burns in their homes.

When lightning strikes a tree, all can see the damage to the outside of the tree. What is not as obvious is the harm done to the inside. Sap heats to the point of boiling. Possible harm may be done to the tree roots. It may take considerable time to see the extent to which the tree was damaged—to see leaves fall off, limbs die, and basic functions of tree life drastically impaired.

When electricity enters a person's body the damage similarly may not be immediately visible. For some survivors, those with a higher voltage injury (for instance, someone who comes in contact with a live electric wire), the power from the electricity usually causes an entrance and exit wound.

Just like the tree, there are visible wounds, such as burned and damaged skin and tissue, and possibly amputations. But also like the tree, there can be internal damage as well—heart problems, nerve damage, memory loss, cataracts, chronic pain, and more. While the injury is not strictly thermal in nature, the energy behind the electricity causes burns all the same. Some electrical injury survivors deal with issues similar to those who experience thermal burn injuries.

Individuals who suffer a lower electrical burn, such as from a household appliance, can also be negatively impacted. Usually, these kinds of injuries do not leave external burns, but the energy that enters the body can cause devastating (though unseen), damage, similar to the damage done to the inside of the tree. This group of low-voltage survivors report symptoms such as memory loss, joint pain, skin sensitivity, change in body temperature (cold and hot), headaches, and sensitivity to light.

Both high and low voltage burn survivors have had their bodies damaged and compromised by the energy and heat of electricity. The road to recovery can be paved with issues that affect the physical, psychological, emotional, relational, spiritual, and financial aspects of life.

In Apartment Buildings

Whether you live in a large apartment complex owned by a major corporation or a single building with only a handful of units, you sign a lease expecting that you will be safe where you live.

No one expects an apartment fire. While tenant-caused accidents do happen, it is generally the responsibility of the landlord to minimize potential fire risks and keep their tenants safe.

A failure by a landlord or a property manager to implement reasonable fire safety precautions may give rise to a claim.

A landlord can and should be responsible for fires in rented apartments or homes. The landlord must assure that smoke detectors, alarms and sprinklers are not only installed, but working.

I asked the Chiefs about apartment living. Interesting to me, almost shockingly, there are not laws in all places requiring sprinklers. The older the building, the less likely there is a sprinkler system, and local and state laws do not always require sprinkler systems, and sometimes, for buildings of an older age, they are "grandfathered," meaning that the laws do not require that they ever be brought "up to code."

Sprinkler systems can be, obviously, the difference between life and death. It amazed me to learn that not every state requires sprinklers in apartments.

One of the Chiefs told me about a legendary Fire Chief, Alan Brunacini, from Phoenix, Arizona. Chief Brunacini has passed, but his legend and influence lives on. Firefighters from all over the country know of him, and his "quotes." The one I liked the best is: "Buildings that God didn't want to burn, he sprinkled."

A Fire Chief at a military base that I interviewed stressed sprinklers as the most important measure for safety. He put if very succinctly: sprinklers save lives, and with them, you have the absolute highest possibility of preventing injury and staying alive.

Another excellent observation involved storage in homes and apartments. Too often apparently, because of a simple lack of space to store "things." Some people crowd otherwise flammable items, such as gas cans or bottles that contain chemicals, in close proximity to each other, or in places that simply aren't safe. These chemicals if mixed together would react, so placing them near each other (and particularly when they are not properly sealed), is a recipe for a fire starting. This Chief told me he has responded to apartment fires (on more than one occasion) because the occupants had placed a motorcycle in their unit's living room.

Kitchen fires, and How to Prevent Burns in the Kitchen

Kitchens are the number one most common starting place for fires in a home. Here are some prevention methods, taken and accumulated from national organizations and fire departments.

1. **Create a kid-free zone.** Teach younger children to stay at least 3 feet away from your cooking space. If you need to watch babies while cooking, place them in a highchair outside of the kid-free zone where you can see them.

2. **Keep hot objects out of children's reach.** Turn pot handles away from the edge. Keep hot foods and liquids away from the edge of your counters and tables.

3. **Use the back burners.** Kids love to reach, so to prevent hot food or liquid spills in the kitchen, simply use the back burner of your stove whenever possible.

4. **Teach older children to cook safely.** Make sure children know not to leave the kitchen while cooking and teach them to always use oven mitts or potholders to carry hot pots and pans.

5. **Avoid using microwaves to heat baby milk or formula.** Microwaves can heat unevenly and create hot spots, so heat bottles by placing them in warm water. Check the temperature using inside of your wrist.

6. **Don't carry or hold a child while cooking.** Instead, move a chair in the kitchen within reach or sight before you start. Then talk to your children, so they know what's going on. It's a great way to spend time together.

Bathtub and Shower Burns, and How to Prevent Scalds

1. Your hot water heater temperature control does not guarantee the temperature of the delivered water! The thermostat at which

the temperature is supposedly set, again, to supposedly tell you what the water temperature will be as delivered, is NOT a good indication of what that delivered water temperature will be. The delivered temperature can vary as much as thirty degrees, meaning if the thermostat setting is 120, the water temperature when first delivered might be 150 degrees. You must get a "regulator" and have your plumber put it on the heater, to assure that the temperature of delivered water does not exceed 120 degrees.

Be aware—clearly—landlords are responsible for this as are water heater manufacturers who do not place regulators on these very dangerous devices!

Further—be aware: children and the elderly will suffer water burns much more quickly than others because their skin is thinner!

2. **Check bathwater temperature.** Before placing your child in the bath, check the water temperature with the inside of your wrist just as you would with baby's milk. The water should feel warm to the touch, not hot.

3. **Place your child in the bath facing away from the water faucet.** This way they won't be tempted to touch the hot faucet or turn on the hot water.

Gas Fireplaces (Hot Glass) Burns and How to Prevent them

1. **Make sure your gas fireplace has a safety screen or safety gate.** These barriers help keep children away from the hot glass on fireplaces. If you need a safety screen, contact the fireplace manufacturer or retailer for the best option for your home.

2. **Keep fireplace remote controls out of children's reach and sight.** Make sure children also stay away from on and off switches for gas fireplaces.

3. **Think about places outside of your home with fireplaces.** When traveling to other homes, restaurants, hotels or resorts, there may not be a safety screen or safety gate installed. Keep children away from the fireplace and teach them not to touch the glass.

Other Areas of the Home Burns and How to Prevent them

1. **Store matches and lighters out of reach.** Teach kids it is not safe to play with matches, lighters or fireworks.

2. **Keep candles at least 12 inches away from anything that can burn.** Blow them out when you leave the room or before you go to sleep

3. **Unplug and safely store irons, flatirons and other appliances.** These appliances can become very hot and take a long time to cool down, so don't leave these appliances unattended when in use. Make sure to turn off and unplug appliances when you are not using them.

4. Place matches, gasoline and lighters in a safe place, out of children's reach. Avoid novelty lighters or lighters that look like toys.

5. Be "alarmed." Install and maintain smoke alarms in your home—on every floor and near every room where family members sleep. Test your smoke alarms once a month to make sure they are working properly. Use long life batteries when possible.

6. Have an escape plan. Create and practice a family fire escape plan and involve kids in the planning. Make sure everyone knows at least two ways out of every room and identify a central meeting place outside.

Chemical Burns

In-home flash fires caused by cleaning liquids, lawn and pool care products, adhesives, and insect repellents are often started by the vapors that are given off by the chemicals in those products.

The majority of residential flash fires (fueled by such products) begin because vapors were accidentally released. Corrosion or puncture of storage containers can allow vapors to be released into the air, which can quickly start a fire if a heat source is present. Products that are kept in a garage or shed may pose an even greater risk because they are often forgotten and may not be properly stored.

Because the vapors travel through the air, flash fires do not always start at the fuel source. For example, the vapors from an improperly stored can of paint thinner that is leaking may reach the nearby pilot light of a water heater. In that case, the extremely hot, quickly moving flash fire will ignite at the heat source and then travel back to the fuel source.

Household product containers should be carefully monitored for leaks. Keeping these products away from heat sources is key to preventing fire. Making sure that the products are being stored in appropriate containers will also reduce the potential of accidental spills.

Containers should be checked, again, for leaks, for corrosion, holes, and properly fitting lids. When products are not in use, lids should be kept on to ensure a tight seal. Safety containers with spring-closing lids that function to relieve internal pressure and prevent spills are available for more highly combustible or flammable products.

Another way to prevent flash fires is by controlling the heat source. When working with open flames, hot surfaces, welding, electricity, or radiant heat, your work area should be free of flammable and combustible materials. Protective gear is also highly recommended to prevent injuries.

You should also work in a well-ventilated area when using cleaning products indoors. Ventilation will not only allow any vapors to dissipate, but will prevent inhalation of vapors, which can cause irritation. A well-ventilated area is crucial to preventing a fire, as well as skin and respiratory irritation.

Using Chemicals as Intended

When flammable or combustible materials are used for purposes other than those intended by the manufacturer, injury is also more likely to occur. According to Jeff Lutz, Fire Marshal for Anaheim (California) Fire & Rescue, "Flash fires that start by using household products incorrectly become intimate fires because of how close people are to the source when the fire starts."

For example, although gasoline is not made for cleaning, it is often used for tasks such as cleaning motor parts because it works well. However, the vapor given off from the gasoline is in direct contact with the user, which can cause significant injuries, should a flash fire occur.

Rags are most commonly used to clean up spills because they are easily accessible to homeowners. However, it is important to then treat those rags as hazardous waste. They should be stored in a noncombustible container, such as a metal coffee can with a sealable lid. Used rags, along with any other hazardous household materials, should always be recycled at your local hazardous-material processing center.

Flash Fire Prevention Tips

Don't use combustible and flammable products near a flame or heat source, such as pilot lights, lit cigarettes, and operating equipment or engines.

Use proper storage containers that prevent leaks and spills.

Keep lids on any chemical products properly closed and sealed.

Clean spills promptly and according to product directions.

Recycle or dispose of hazardous household materials at your local hazardous material processing center.

Don't store hazards inside your home.

Keep hazardous products out of reach of children—call poison control in the event of accidental ingestion or exposure,

B) At Work

Workplace accidents account for 8% of burn injuries, and men are most likely to be burned from fire, scalds, chemical and electrical burns. The information currently available from the **Occupational Safety and Health Administration** (OSHA) shows that more than 5,000 burn injuries occur in the United States annually from work-related fires and explosions.

Burns in the workplace are a major threat to individuals, families, and the community as a whole. Plant workers, electricians, and other persons exposed to the hazards of dangerous chemicals and high voltage are at risk for chemical and electrical burns. These burn injuries can be devastating and life altering.

There are several types of common workplace burns:

Thermal burns—these burns, also called "scalding burns," caused by the heat from liquids, hot objects, open flames, and explosions. The immediate objective with thermal burns is to contain and stop the burning process. Thermal burns and injuries can be prevented by wearing personal protective equipment, by having established emergency procedures in place related to fire detection and protection, and by using fire prevention tactics.

Chemical burns—Chemical burns occur when eyes or skin come into contact with any caustic material that destroys or "burns" skin and deeper tissue. They commonly occur in the workplace following exposure to industrial cleansers, for chemicals used in laboratories or in the manufacturing process. Employers should make sure that all of their workers have proper training and that they receive ongoing training in Hazard Communication. Workers must be able to assimilate, read, and understand all symbols and labels that identify chemical risk.

Electrical Burns—Electrical burns start at electrical sources, high-voltage areas, and machinery. These burns see electric currents traveling through the body and meeting resistance in tissues, resulting in heat burn injuries. To minimize this risk, workers should be on the lookout for and should identify live wires, avoid contact with water while working with electricity, and wear personal protective equipment.

My biggest takeaway from listening to the military Fire Chief was about the redoing of commercial spaces, such as making a warehouse into an office building. In this and other re-purposing, the question becomes one of examining the original intended use, understanding the likelihood of problems that can occur if there are not enough or proper exits, or ramps, or stairwells, and involving building inspectors and fire prevention personnel to be involved in the remodeling process. Moreover, examination of the building's electric capacity and assurance of not overloading the new space is vital

Work Accidents—2 possible claims: Worker's Compensation and "Third Party"

If a worker suffers a burn at work, the employer is responsible. Usually then, "worker's compensation" takes over and assists the injured worker. All states have a process for workers injured while working, called "worker's compensation claims." This claims process prohibits claims directly against the employer, but happily, the process eliminates any conversation or discussion about "fault." The worker's compensation system normally completely addresses the various claims, including medical bills, lost wages, and potential permanent injuries. Notwithstanding that this type of claim is "automatic," survivors are urged to retain an attorney competent in burn injuries and worker's compensation claims, because these claims are typically "downplayed" by worker's compensation insurance companies, who often stall, delay and deny otherwise legitimate claims. It will take the knowledge and skill of an attorney to fight for, and hopefully obtain appropriate compensation for the survivor.

If a worker suffers an injury while working, and the cause of the burn injury is the failure of a machine, apparatus, or some party other than the employer, a "third party" claim might be made, in addition to the worker's compensation claim. The survivor has two claims. The first, as discussed above, is the worker's compensation claim, and the second is the claim against the responsible party.

The award in a worker's compensation claim is typically much lower than what that in a traditional personal injury civil lawsuit. The standards of compensation vary from state to state, but if a plaintiff is not seriously injured or disabled by the injury and does not have disfiguring scars, the worker's compensation payment may not be very high.

For example, a worker who receives second and third degree burns on his lower legs with some scarring, but is not otherwise disabled or impaired, might not expect to receive a very significant amount of monetary compensation.

Worker's compensation laws are quite complex and therefore the services of an experienced attorney are typically required to obtain a successful result.

Safety in the Workplace

When it comes to burns, here is more detail for the way employers can help to provide safe workplaces.

Initial Training

Making sure employees have the proper training is one of the most important steps an employer can take. Training should cover not only the hazards that the employee might face on their worksite, but also an overview of OSHA standards and how to identify hazards that may not have been covered. OSHA 10-hour training is a great way to get a baseline of safety standards training before an employee even begins receiving worksite-specific training. Then, employers should make sure that the employees are trained on their specific job functions, including in-depth safety training with any machinery, chemicals or other worksite hazards specific to their job.

Refresher Training

In addition to training before starting a job, employers should regularly update training so that employees are kept current and so that important concepts are kept at top-of-mind. Certificate training courses are a great way to re-train employees.

Hazard Communication

Color codes, posters, labels or signs to warn employees of potential hazards are an employer requirement under the OSHA **Globally Harmonized System** (GHS) of Classification and Labeling of Chemicals Act, and these vital pieces of Hazard Communication are extremely important in burn prevention. Workers should be trained to recognize symbols and other hazard communication codes, and GHS communication standards should be used to identify material hazards in a consistent and easily recognizable way. When hazardous chemicals are used in the workplace, employers are also required to produce and provide a written Hazard Communication plan.

C) Burn Injuries From Automobile / Traffic Accidents

Traffic accidents can cause burn injuries to motorists. When a vehicle's airbag deploys during a traffic accident it comes out of the dashboard at an extremely high speed. The airbag will also be hot. Further, airbag chemicals often assist in the deployment. While airbags undeniably save lives and prevent many car accident injuries, they can also be the cause of injuries to drivers and passengers. While rare, those injuries can be serious. They can leave survivors with lifelong scars or permanent disfigurement.

If a vehicle's gas tank is punctured in an automobile accident or if a flammable liquid reacts with a heat source, an accident can quickly go from dangerous to deadly. Automotive explosions can result in permanent, life-altering injuries and even death.

About Air Bag Burns

Air bag temperatures can reach 500 degrees Celsius when deployed. Burns may occur from direct contact with hot air bags.

Drivers may be vulnerable to burns on their hands and forearms due to the placement of air bags (side, steering wheel) and vents that release hot gas into the car.

Hot venting gases can also cause clothes to melt onto the body, particularly lightweight synthetics.

Air bag burns also can happen as a side effect of the inflation process. Chemicals from the air bag can cause eye damage, even potential blindness. The devices can also cause thermal burns from the high temperatures reached by gases and the possibility of melting clothing. Researchers have found that burn injuries caused by air bags most often affect the face, hands, chest, and arms.

Potential defendants in a lawsuit for an airbag injury case are usually:

* The automobile manufacturer
* The airbag manufacturer
* Whoever did the inspection, maintenance, or replacement of the car's airbag after purchase
* The driver who hit you

What Should You Do If You Think an Airbag Malfunctioned?

The most important thing after an accident is to preserve the evidence related to the airbag.

* Keep a copy of the police report generated after the accident
* Save any information provided by the car or airbag manufacturer
* Do not let the airbag be thrown away after the accident
* Make sure that you do not let the car be junked or transferred to the insurance company.

Vehicle Fires

Vehicle fires were responsible for 17% of fire deaths in 2019. Fires involving vehicles may occur because of poor maintenance, defective vehicle parts, or car accidents. Young children and older adults may become quickly overwhelmed by smoke inhalation. They may also have a more difficult time escaping a house or vehicle fire than younger or middle-aged adults due to size and mobility. Vehicle fires cause an average of 490 deaths and 1,275 injuries each year.

CHAPTER **4**

Special Considerations for Children

This chapter is a summary of literature from numerous medical care centers, organizations and foundations, including information from psychology resources.

One of the worst fears a parent can have is seeing their child injured and suffering. With burn injuries, your child likely experienced immense pain due to someone else's carelessness. You're angry, but most of all, you're concerned. You want to ease the pain and provide your child with the best possible means of recovery.

Working through the trauma and continuing trauma of a burn injury to your child is probably going to be challenging for your entire family.

From the **Montreal Children's Patient and Family Centered Care Policy:**

Family-centered care is based on the belief that the family is a child's primary source of strength and support. Healthcare professionals are the experts on health and disease. Parents are the experts on their children, and they can offer essential information to enhance their child's health care. A successful partnership between healthcare providers and families is based on mutual trust, respect and responsibility.

Family members and parents then are an integral part of the team, and therefore should accompany the child during all procedures. The presence of parents will reassure and comfort the child, and it will allow the parents to see the evolution of the healing process.

Some of the issues and problems child burn survivors may have to face include:

- The loss of their prior appearance
- The loss of their pre-injury lifestyle and recreational activities

- The loss of a limb or limited mobility and range of motion
- The loss of certain dreams and hopes for their future
- The loss of other loved ones or pets in the accident that caused their injuries
- The loss of their home and possessions
- The loss of friends and family relationships

The following has been taken from the Phoenix Society's website and is included here for its excellent treatment of concerns for children and teens who have suffered burn injuries.

COMMON MANIFESTATIONS OF TRAUMA IN YOUNG CHILDREN: (APPROXIMATELY 2–6 YR.)

Generalized fear and anxiety

Nightmares, night terrors, fear of going to sleep or sleeping alone

Regressive behaviors, (bed-wetting, talking baby talk, thumb sucking, whining)

Repetitive trauma play, may have difficulty verbalizing about the trauma

Confusion and difficulty understanding that the trauma is over

Attachment anxiety, (clinging, excessive concern about parent leaving)

Physical symptoms, (stomachaches, headaches, other physical symptoms)

Personality changes, may be withdrawn and passive, or aggressive and reckless

School difficulty, such as difficulty concentrating may not want to go to school

Arguing, fighting, agitated, restless, quick to anger and become defensive

MANIFESTATIONS IN OLDER CHILDREN: (APPROXIMATELY 6–12 YR.)

Fears are more specific and related to the trauma

Sleep disturbance, (nightmares, fear of sleeping alone)

Obsessing about and talking about the trauma repeatedly, compulsive behaviors

Guilt related to not being able to control the trauma

Impaired ability to concentrate and learn

Changes in behavior, (such as withdrawn and isolating, or aggressive and reckless)

Feeling overwhelmed by and afraid of losing control of feelings

Concern for the safety of family members

Fear of death and sometimes a fear of spirits or ghosts

MANIFESTATIONS IN ADOLESCENTS: (APPROXIMATELY 12–18 YR.)

May include symptoms of older children, as well as adult symptoms

May be self-conscious about feelings, fears, and being different

Aggressive, destructive, self-destructive, risk taking, acting out behaviors, (substance abuse, sexual acting out, delinquent behavior, truancy, etc.)

Avoidance of interpersonal relationships, withdrawal, social isolation

Personality changes, depression, apathy, moodiness

Leaving school or leaving home, or fear of separating from family/ parents

Pessimism, cynicism, plans of revenge

Failing grades, disinterest in school, friends, and previously enjoyed activities

The following behaviors are common after loss. It is when these behaviors persist for months after the loss that they are considered red flags and indicate the need for professional assessment and intervention.

Most articles and publications about burn injury recovery, and most experts, will tell you that many burn survivors believe that their situation will be significantly better when "coming home from the hospital." This is particularly true for children coming home. While that concept certainly has some truth, as home is always preferred to being in a hospital, often, unfortunately, there is still a-ways to go once home.

The coming home process all starts before you even leave the hospital.

- First, make sure the home recovery room is clear and free of any potential obstacles, such as throw rugs that can slip. Cover all aspects of home care with the *burn team* and practice them thoroughly before you leave the hospital.

- Learn exactly how best to care for your child's healing skin; practice the correct washing protocol and massage technique to soothe and alleviate itchiness. Newly healed skin can be hypersensitive to heat and cold, and you may need to learn how to best regulate both body and room temperature.

- If your child needs pressure garments, learn how to dress, change, and launder them. Depending upon the extent of a child's injuries, consider involving a **physiotherapist**, whose job is to evaluate the child's ability to move his or her body, to prevent scar contracture and to help restore normal range of motion (ROM) of the involved joints to assist in achieving the highest level of function. The physiotherapist will concentrate on gross motor function, including gait training, stairs, balance, coordination, and strengthening and improving cardiovascular endurance. Recommendations for equipment are made as needed.

- A Speech and Language pathologist should be involved when there are inhalation burn injuries. Often there are problems communicating due to injury to the vocal tract and/or the vocal cords. The pathologist may be involved from early-on when the child is intubated and alert. The pathologist can help establish a personalized method of non-verbal communication, such as something as simple as a pad of paper and pen or pencil. Electronic tablets are now being used for those old enough to communicate in that fashion.

- A psychologist should be considered to regain any loss or lapse in self-esteem or confidence. Psychological symptoms can impair social functioning in school and at home. Nightmares and flashbacks can be difficult to manage. Treatment is recommended when symptoms affect the child's functioning or influence behavior.

- Nutrition is a key factor in recovery, and children need energy in the form of high-calorie and high protein to give them the extra calories needed for recovery. **Talk to your burn team about specific foods your child should have and involve a nutritionist.**

- Prevent Contractures. A contracture is a serious complication of a burn injury. They develop when a burn scar matures, thickens or tightens preventing or limiting movement. A contracture prevents moving the scarred area normally. The effort to prevent contractures involves having the child perform normal daily activities as much as possible, such as eating, brushing teeth and hair, as well as getting dressed. It is important to encourage the child to continue doing these things despite that they may find them challenging.

It is essential that you establish a daily routine, and build independence in your child, while simultaneously assuring your child of your love and commitment. Maintain the same rules and expectations after the injury as you did before the injury. Try not to allow normal feelings of sadness or guilt to affect your parenting style; make exceptions occasionally or bend the rules of the household.

Encourage your child to feel like a survivor. Stress how strong they are, and constantly express your love, and reaffirm the inherent strength you know he or she has to get through the healing process and back to normal. It is vital to incorporate your child's treatment into your regular family routine, without focusing family life on the treatment.

Children have less experience and ability to cope with stress, so be alert to any signs indicating an adjustment problem. Withdrawal, depression, aggression, frustration, nightmares, or changes in any bodily functions, are just some of the symptoms to monitor. You many need to enlist help from a *medical professional* should any changes in behavior occur.

As your child's most ardent *advocate*, you're fighting on many fronts. Try to take as good care of yourself as you are giving your child by getting as much sleep, nutrition, and exercise as possible. Making time for yourself and your needs will enable you to better support your child, and your child will play off your cues.

The most successful prescription for your child's complete recovery at home is to manage pain, promote physical healing, address all emotional needs, and bolster your child's self-confidence and strength. It takes equal measures of careful planning, time, and patience. If all conditions are ultimately met, your entire family will not only be burn survivors, but also victors who by virtue of this shared, life-changing experience, are able to successfully manage the inevitable challenges that life brings.

Problems or issues to look out for

You should contact your doctor or burn center facility where your child received care if any of these occur:

- Fever from burns
- Increase in wound pain

- Wound odor
- Bleeding from the wound between dressing changes
- Increased swelling to the burn injured part of the body

Plan school reentry

Although you or your child may be nervous about school reentry, do not avoid the subject. Discuss returning to school as soon as possible to allow him time to get used to the idea. Also, be sure to contact your child's school and involve staff members in his reentry.

Allow your child to express himself, but do not press the issue. Understand that your child may act differently after his injury. Allow him to express himself and let him know that he can always talk to you about his injuries and feelings, but do not pressure him to talk if he is not yet comfortable.

Returning to school most probably will be challenging, and even frightening. Nonetheless, it is beneficial (and needed) for children to return to their academic and social activities as soon as they can. To help with this transition, a member of a psychological team can go to the school in advance to help prepare classmates and teachers for your child's return. This often helps students understand burn trauma and to recognize what their classmate has experienced. It also provides an excellent opportunity to discuss burn prevention.

Explore support groups and therapy in your area

You may also want to look into therapy—both for your child and the rest of the family. Consider whether you think group therapy or one-on-one therapy would be best for your child.

Burn Camps for Children

The International Association of Burn Camps (IABC) provides a network for the mutual benefit of local and regional organizations that serve the burn community. These camps support the physical, social, and psychological needs of burn survivors and their families. For more information, log on to: *http://www.iaburncamps.org/membership/member-camps/*

Consider these tips for helping your child cope with loss but remember that these tips may not be appropriate for children of all ages. Work with professional to find age-appropriate options.

Children's Sleepwear/Pressure Garments

Children's sleepwear is any article of clothing, such as a nightgown, pajama, robe or loungewear, that is sized above 9 months and up to size 14 and that is intended to be worn primarily for sleeping or activities related to sleeping.

To determine whether a garment is sleepwear, the Commission considers:

1. The nature of the garment and its suitability for sleeping or activities related to sleeping;

2. How the garment is promoted and distributed; and

3. The likelihood that the garment will be used by children primarily for sleeping or activities related to sleeping in a substantial number of cases. Underwear and diapers are not children's sleepwear. A garment sized nine months or smaller intended for use by infants is not required to meet the standard if:

    (1) It is a one-piece garment and is not longer than 25¾ inches, or it is a two-piece garment and has no piece longer than 15 ¾ inches; and

    (2) It has a label stating in months the age of the children for whom it is intended. Even though these types of garments are exempt from the requirements of this rule, they must still meet the flammability requirements for clothing textiles.

What is the purpose of the children's sleepwear flammability standards?

Children's sleepwear must be flame resistant and self-extinguish if a flame from a candle, match, lighter or a similar item causes it to catch fire. All children's sleepwear above size 9 months and up to size 14 require that:

1. the fabric and garments pass certain flammability tests; or

2. be "tight fitting" as defined by specified dimensions

CHAPTER **5**

Sample Burn Injury Verdicts

Case "values"—meaning the amount of compensation a burn survivor "gets"—will vary as widely as injuries and as widely as the composition of juries in courtrooms all over the country. What can be gleaned from this sampling of cases, however, is that burn injuries tend to be compensated highly, evidencing the widespread understanding of how truly horrible and serious these injuries truly are.

Case values may also depend upon the extent of investigation, and the evidence that is shown to a jury. As well, the skill of an attorney in fully and properly representing his or her is always a factor, but, a bad result does not always mean the attorney did not do a proper job.

Construction Worker/Electrical Wire
McGee v. The City of Alameda, California / $25 million settlement

A construction worker hit an underground, energized electrical line while using a drill at a construction site, causing him severe electrical injuries that resulted in third degree burns to over 20 percent of his body, several amputations.

Fraternity House University Student/Firecracker
Doe Individual v. Doe University Fraternity House, Philadelphia / $5.2 million settlement

A university student was severely burned when fellow fraternity members threw a firecracker into the room of a fraternity house where he was sleeping.

Water and Power Employee/Power Pole Electric Burns
Doe Individual v. Doe Cable Company, Lexington, KY / $2.1 million settlement

Department of Water and Power employee was electrocuted, severely burning his hands, while working on a power pole transmitter. The transmitter was inadvertently grounded as a result of the negligent stringing of a cable TV line.

Refinery Worker/Pressurized Liquid Escaped
Younger v. Foster Wheeler Settlement, California /
$1.75 million settlement

Thirty-six-year-old refinery worker was severely burned when pressurized liquid escaped from a negligently designed cooker at an oil refinery in Torrance.

Patron using Microwave/Interlock System Failure
Canela v. Tom's Vending Company Settlement, San Francisco /
$1 million settlement

Plaintiff opened the door of a microwave oven mid-cycle to rotate his food. The interlock system failed and caused deep burns to the nerves and muscles of plaintiff's major hand.

Child/Fire Pot Explosion
Wahl v. Armstrong Home and Gardens and TJ Maxx, California /
Confidential Settlements

Minor Delaney Wahl suffered severe burn injuries from an outdoor fire pot that exploded due to defects in the design of the fire pot and the fuel gel used to fill the fire pot. Discovery revealed that TJ Maxx had known of the defects in the fuel gel for over a year prior to the explosion and had conducted a secret internal recall of the product without alerting its customers.

Auto Accident, truck hit power line/No Safety Devices
Alpert v. Will-Burt: Confidential Settlement, Mississippi / $1.5 million settlement

KABC-TV reporter Adrienne Alpert was severely burned and electrified by power lines her mobile transmission truck hit while covering a news story. Equipment was not fitted with necessary safety devices.

Child in Apartment Basement/Gasoline Explosion
Minor, Doe v. Landlord, New Hampshire / $300,000 settlement

The case involved a 13-year-old boy who was severely burned in a gasoline explosion and fire. The boy entered the basement without the landlord's permission (allegedly). He said he was going to get his bike. No bikes were in the basement. He then knocked over a can of gas which was ignited by the water heater.

Construction Worker, Auto Accident/Vehicle Explosion
Hawthorne v. Vehicle Asset Universal Trust, Queens County / $10 million verdict, reduced to $2.5 million

A 40-year-old construction worker was literally burned alive in his car when he could not escape after a motor vehicle accident. Hawthorne sustained deep burns of his entire body and endured 10 minutes of conscious pain and suffering before death. A Queens County jury awarded Mr. Stanton's estate $10,000,000 for his pain and suffering but the trial judge found that the jury had been over-emotional and rendered an excessive award. The judge ordered a reduction to $2,500,000.

Surgery Patient/Operating Room Light Failure
Paruolo v Yormak, Westchester County, NY / $425,000 verdict

A 50-year-old school guidance counselor suffered from elbow pain that was ultimately diagnosed as a chondral injury requiring surgery to remove loose bone fragments. During the surgery, an operating room light was negligently maintained and caused third degree burns on Mr. Paruolo's elbow and arm. He didn't even know he had burn injuries until there days after surgery when his bandages were removed and there was visible blistering. He had infections, underwent six days of hospitalization to administer antibiotics and he needed a debridement and skin graft from his thigh.

The court was moved by the facts that plaintiff had two permanent and embarrassing scars on his elbow and thigh, the scars could not be exposed to sunlight and posed a heightened risk of skin cancer, he had to wear long sleeve shirts in warm weather and would suffer from all of these for the remainder of his life.

Apartment Tenant/Defective Gas Valve in Dryer, explosion
Ramirez v. Westwind Development Inc., Texas / $6.9 million verdict

An improperly installed gas valve for dryer resulted in an explosion causing second degree burns to 20% of Plaintiff's body. The burns permanently scarred his face. He also injured his hip and back and had to undergo surgery.

Auto Accident/Vehicle explosion
Brown v. City of Chicago / $530,000 verdict

Plaintiff received third degree burns to the side of her head, neck and shoulders from accident involving police car.

Firefighter/Defective Safety Alert System (alarm)
Dryer v. City Lanes LLC, New York / $10.5 million verdict

A firefighter's safety alert system did not work as it should and the alarm failed to go off. As a result, he suffered third and fourth degree burns to various parts of his body. The fourth degree burns necessitated amputation of his right arm.

Worker/Electrical Panel Defective AND Fire Extinguisher Empty
Martinez v. Brownco, California / $3.188 million verdict

The plaintiff was at work when an electrical panel engulfed him in a fireball. As if the explosion and initial injury were not bad enough, the nearby fire extinguisher was empty. The Plaintiff sustained second and third degree burns to nearly 40% of his body surface. After over a month in intensive care and burn units with his loving wife by his side, and many more months of therapy and treatment, Mr. Martinez's case was brought to a Los Angeles courtroom and was tried before a jury. After a 21-day jury trial, the jury returned a verdict in Mr. and Mrs. Martinez' favor of approximately $3.188 million.

3 Workers/Water Heater Explosion
3 Workers v. Water Heater Company, Miami, FL / $2.7 million settlement

A faulty water heater injured two workers and killed one. The heater stopped functioning and emitted toxic gases. Those caught on fire and caused an explosion. One man died from his injuries. A second had third degree burns over most of his body. The third man had burns over a small portion of his body. The estate of the man who died settled for $600,000 because his wife needed the money to take care of four children. The worker with significant burns settled for $1.6 million, and the third man settled for $500,000.

Student/Chemistry Demonstration
10th grade student v. NY School System, Manhattan, NY / $60 million verdict

A Manhattan judge upheld a jury's verdict of $60 million in pain and suffering damages awarded to a former 10th-grade student who was "literally … burned alive" inside a massive fireball that leapt from a chemistry teacher's nitrate-demonstration gone wrong.

From a national publication: Jury Verdict Research / November, 2003 Statistics:

Jury Verdict Research Releases Burn-Injury Verdict-Study: Juries Award at Least $1 Million in 96% of 'Catastrophic Burn Injuries' Cases

Plaintiffs who sued and won claiming catastrophic burn injuries received a jury award of at least $1 million in close to 100% of the cases, according to Jury Verdict Research's report, *Nationwide Trends in Burn Injury Verdicts and Settlements.*

CHAPTER 6

Resources—Foundations and Organizations, Medical Care Centers (Burn Centers), Burn Camps, Products for Survivors

This chapter is included to be as complete a resource for those who have been burned, and for survivors and their families, as possible. It is divided into four sections as detailed in the title. Contact information is provided, and where available, information as well.

The Medical Care Centers—Hospitals or Burn Centers, are listed alphabetically by state, as are the Burn Camps.

A) Foundations and Organizations

American Burn Association
311 S. Wacker Drive # 4150
Chicago, IL 60606-6671
312-642-9260
www.ameriburn.org

"With more than 2,000 members worldwide, we dedicate our efforts and resources to promoting and supporting burn-related care, prevention, education, and research. Our multidisciplinary membership enhances our ability to work toward common goals with other organizations and educational programs."

Phoenix Society for Burn Survivors
525 Ottawa Avenue, NW FRNT
Grand Rapids, MI 49503
800-888-2876
info@phoenix-society.org
https://www.phoenix-society.org/

Founded by Alan Breslau in 1977, Phoenix Society serves burn survivors, loved ones, burn care professionals, researchers, and anyone else committed to empowering the burn community and building a safer world. It is the leading national nonprofit organization dedicated to empowering people affected by a burn injury. Alan, who was a burn survivor from a 1963 airplane crash recognized the transformative power of peer support.

Phoenix Society Burn Congress

The Phoenix Society's World Burn Congress offers a unique atmosphere of burn survivors, families, healthcare providers, burn professionals, and firefighters who come together as one caring community of support. People come to learn, grow and share their amazing experiences. Many people have described the experience as a life-changing moment in their lives. It is a forum for encouraging and facilitating the sharing of stories, providing support and increasing knowledge of burn recovery. Whether you are a survivor, parent of a survivor, or a family member/caregiver you will find that World Burn Congress offers a healing environment for all. To learn more about the Phoenix Society and the Virtual World Burn Congress , visit *https://www.phoenix-society.org/phoenix-wbc.*

Author's Note: The Phoenix Society, and the next organization, the Alissa Alan Ruch Burn Foundation, are truly sensational, top-notch organizations. I highly recommend any who are interested in information start with either of these groups.

Alissa Alan Ruch Burn Foundation
50 N. Hill Avenue, Suite 305
Pasadena, CA
1-800-242-BURN
info@aarbf.org
https://www.aarbf.org/

Founded in 1971, the Foundation works in partnership with firefighters, educators, and burn care professionals to develop innovative programs and services. Their mission is to significantly reduce the number of burn injuries through prevention education, and to enhance the quality of life of those affected by burn injuries in California.

Burncare... Everywhere Foundation, Inc.
283 Tarrytown Road
White Plains, NY 10607
914-224-3008
www.burncarefoundation.org

Provides national funding for acute care, rehabilitation, and recon-structive burn medicine. The Burn Care Foundation is a division of MercyCare Inc., national non-profit organization dedicated to assisting accident and trauma patients in obtaining specialty medical care for their injuries.

Moonlight Fund
Bandara Office
PO Box 1299
Bandara, TX 78003
210-415-3406
info@moonlightfund.org
https://moonlightfund.org/

Moonlight Fund actively raises money throughout the year in an effort to support those with financial needs (such as gaps in medical care, reha-bilitation services, burial expenses, housing, and transportation needs). Additional services include child care assistance, tuition expenses, and referrals to third party support services. The Fund is open to any request. We do ask that all requests be made in writing by the attending physi-cian, case worker, or qualified rehabilitation or educational facility.

Moonlight Fund offers retreats several times a year at the Silver Spur Ranch in Bandera, TX. The 4-day gatherings offer an opportunity for those with recent burn injuries to spend time with fellow long-term survivors. The retreat offers alternative healing methods and emotional support to both patients and family members. It's a traditional dude ranch experience with horseback riding and true western culture.

Burn Foundation of America
3614 J. Dewey Gray Circle, Building C
Augusta, GA 30909
(706) 855-2876
info@sfbf.net
https://www.burnfoundation.net/

The Burn Foundation of America provides assistance to families of burn patients being treated at the Joseph M. Still Burn Center at Doctors Hospital, in Augusta, Georgia. This includes lodging at the Chavis House, daily meals and transportation—all free of charge. In addition, the Burn Foundation assists patients upon their discharge with services related to their return to independent living. This includes providing medications, anti-scarring garments and transportation for follow up medical visits.

Children's Burn Foundation
5000 Van Nuys Boulevard
Suite 450
Sherman Oaks, CA 91403
(818) 907-2822
https://www.charitynavigator.org/

The Children's Burn Foundation is dedicated to providing support services for child burn survivors, from infancy to age 18 and their families, as well as burn prevention and fire safety education to thousands of children and caregivers in Southern California, nationally, and internationally. The Children's Burn Foundation is concerned with the full recovery of a child burn survivor, where addressing not only their patient's physical needs, but their psychological, emotional, and social recovery as well is top priority. "We are the only known foundation that offers the Full Recovery Program for child burn survivors, locally, nationally, and internationally—a unique blend of medical care, psycho-social support services, and daily living support to help young burn survivors achieve their full potential."

Knapp Burn Foundation
PO Box 1135
Bloomington, IL 61702
309-663-1008
info@knapp-burn.org
https://www.knapp-burn.org/

The Knapp Burn Foundation was established in 1989,by the family and friends of a burn survivor injured in 1975. Throughout the surgery and rehabilitation, they realized just how much pain and suffering not only the burn survivors endured, but that their families also experienced. While reflecting on that time of our lives, we came to the realization that current support systems are not enough to cope with the losses suffered through burns. Therefore, the Knapp Burn Foundation was created as a not-for-profit organization committed to:

1. Assisting burn victims and their families through the temporary and/or permanent physical, social, economic and emotional challenges.

2. Advocating for and assimilating burn survivors to return to socially fulfilling and occupationally productive lives.

3. Educating and equipping the public with burn information.

"We strive to provide the support and resources to allow burn survivors to move beyond their burns and continue with their lives, and promote burn prevention and awareness." Some of the Knapp Burn Foundation's most requested and rewarding programs are:

- John Bennett-Saviano Educational Grant

- John A. James Garment Grant

- Working with fire and medical professionals to understand the lifelong commitments of survivors and their families.

- Sponsoring community projects and educating schools on burn awareness and prevention.

- Being available.

Burn Foundation
8600 West Chester Pike, Suite 202
Upper Darby, PA 19082-2629
(215) 545- 3816
(484) 454- 5367
info@burnfoundation.org
https://burnfoundation.org/

To serve the Greater Philadelphia Area-Delaware Valley, including Southeastern PA, Southern NJ and the state of DE, in supporting burn survivors to enhance their quality of life and that of their families. Their purpose is to be a well known, first-rate regional resource for the burn care and patient communities and fire service industry. Their focus is in the areas of prevention, education, treatment and recovery.

Global Medical Relief Fund
112 MacFarland Ave.
Staten Island, NY 10305
718-448-6984
info@gmrfchildren.org
https://gmrfchildren.org/

The Global Medical Relief Fund was established in 1977, and along with partners, doctors, nurses and hospitals and volunteer have given aid to more than 375 children who are missing or have lost the use of limbs or eyes, have been severely burned, or have been injured due to war, natural disaster or illness.

National Fire Protection Association (NFPA)
1 Batterymarch Park
Quincy, Massachusetts
02169-7471
+1 800 344-3555 (U.S. & Canada)
+1 855 274-8525 (U.S. & Canada)
+1 617 770-3000 (International)
custserv@nfpa.org
https://www.nfpa.org/

The National Fire Protection Association established in 1896, is a global nonprofit organization, devoted to eliminating death, injury, property and economic loss due to fire, electrical and related hazards. NFPA delivers information and knowledge through more than 300 consensus codes and standards, research, training, education, outreach and advocacy, and by partnering with others who share an interest in furthering the mission. NFPA membership totals more than 60,000 individuals around the world.

Burned Children Recovery Foundation
409 Wood Place
Everett, WA 98203, USA
1-800-799-BURN (2876)
burnedchildrenrecovery@gmail.com
https://www.burnedchildrenrecovery.org/

The Burn Children Recovery Foundation, founded in 1989, are committed to a single goal; a national recovery agency that has provided emotional support and financial aid to burned children and their families. They believe every burned child should have an opportunity to heal from both physical and emotional injuries. The foundation strives to offer these children from all socio-economic backgrounds these opportunities. With the help of financial assistance, they are able to bring children (and family members) to Phoenix House for immediate support as well as provide children a Camp experience (Camp Phoenix) to meet other children and engage in meaningful learning and friendship environment.

IAFF Disaster Relief Fund
1750 New York Ave NW, Suite 300
Washington, DC 20006
202-737-8484
https://foundation.iaff.org/disaster-relief/

When there's a national emergency or natural disaster—from hurricanes, wildfires, floods and tornadoes to mass casualty events and civil disturbances—fire fighters and paramedics remain on the frontlines serving their communities. And when they—and their families—are victims of these events or experience loss, the IAFF Foundation provides disaster relief, including financial relief, food, water and other supplies, clothing and shelter, medical aid, behavioral health counseling and more. In sacrificing their lives to save others, fallen fire fighters often leave a family behind.

The IAFF Foundation provides scholarships to children of IAFF members who make the ultimate sacrifice. Every year, the Foundation helps more than 40 students pay for post-secondary education. It is through the Foundation that we provide support to the families who attend the IAFF Fallen Fire Fighter Memorial annual observance. From the flags to transportation to the medals we give to those who've lost a loved one, the Foundation makes sure that the families are taken care of throughout the memorial service weekend. When an IAFF member or family member suffers a burn injury, the Foundation provides financial assistance and a peer support network to ensure they receive proper care and treatment with their families by their side. The Foundation also holds the International Burn Camp each year in Washington, DC. The week-long camp is a life-changing opportunity for teenage burn survivors and the fire fighter camp counselors who work to make a difference in the lives of these young people.

Spiegel Burn Foundation
2251 N. Rampart #157
Las Vegas, NV 89128
702-491-3987
julie@spiegelburnfoundation.com
https://www.spiegelburnfoundation.com/

Provides advocacy support and services to assist burn victims and their family members. As a private nonprofit foundation, we provide:

- Attendee grants to The World Burn Congress*
- Support for complementary alternative medical modalities
- Grants for research and special needs related to Burn Survivors

Our focus is on assisting survivors of burns and burn related injuries to learn to live with many of the new concerns and issues that are now before them. Most people don't realize that scars of a serious burn injury never go away. The physical, emotional and economic damage can, and often do, last a lifetime.

Arizona Burn Foundation
1432 N. 7th St.
Phoenix, AZ 85006
602-230-2041
https://azburn.org/

The Arizona Burn Foundation was founded in 1967 by two Maricopa County surgeons and an attorney: Dr. MacDonald Wood and Dr. William Price, and George Randolph. For more than 50 years, they have provided high-quality support programs for Arizona children and adult burn survivors and their families. In 1991, they launched Camp Courage, and in 2001 they opened their first Forever Courage House to provide housing support to survivors' families while in recovery at the hospital.

B) Medical Care Centers / Burn Centers
Arizona
Arizona Burn Center at Maricopa Medical Center
2601 E. Roosevelt Street
Phoenix, AZ 85008
602-344-5726
https://valleywisehealth.org/arizona-burn-center-valleywise-health/

California
LAC + USC Medical Center
2051 Marengo Street
Los Angeles, CA 90033
323-409-1000
https://dhs.lacounty.gov/lacusc/

UCI Regional Burn Center
Building 1, 101 The City Drive S.
Orange, CA 92868
888-622-2876
http://www.ucihealth.org/medical-services/burn-center

Shriners Hospital for Children-Northern California Pediatric Burn Center
2425 Stockton Blvd.
Sacramento, CA 95817
916-453-2000
https://www.shrinershospitalsforchildren.org/sacramento/burn-care

UC Davis Regional Burn Center
2315 Stockton Blvd.
Sacramento, CA 95817
916-453-2050
https://health.ucdavis.edu/burncenter/contactus/index.html

UC San Diego Regional Burn Center
200 West Arbor Drive
San Diego, CA 92103
619-543-6505
https://health.ucsd.edu/specialties/burn-center/Pages/default.aspx

Bothin Burn Center
900 Hyde Street
San Francisco, CA 94109
415-353-6255
https://www.dignityhealth.org/bayarea/locations/saintfrancis/services/ bothin-burn-center

Santa Clara Valley Medical Burn Center
751 S Bascom Avenue
San Jose, CA 95128
408-885-6670
https://www.scvmc.org/health-care-services/Burn-Center/Pages/Over- view.aspx

Torrance Memorial Medical Burn Center
3325 Medical Center Drive West, Tower, 5th Floor
Torrance, CA 90505
310-517-4736
https://www.torrancememorial.org/Medical_Services/Burn_Wound_ and_Amputation_Prevention_Center.aspx

Grossman Burn Center
7325 Medical Center Drive #200
West Hills, CA 91307
888-676-2876
https://westhillshospital.com/service/grossman-burn-center

Colorado
University of Colorado Hospital Burn Center
12605 E. 16th Avenue Anschutz Inpatient Pavilion, 3rd floor
Aurora, CO 80045
720-848-0747
https://www.uchealth.org/locations/uchealth-burn-center-anschutz-medical-campus/

Connecticut
The Burn Center at Bridgeport Hospital
267 Grant Street
Bridgeport, CT 06610
203-384-3728
https://www.bridgeporthospital.org/services/trauma-burn/ct-burn-center.aspx

District of Columbia, Washington
The Burn Center at MedStar Washington Hospital Center
10 Irving Street, NW
Washington, DC 20010
202-877-7347
https://www.medstarwashington.org/our-services/emergency-trauma-and-burn-care/treatments/the-burn-center/

Florida
University of Florida Burn Center
1600 SW Archer Road, Room 7209
Gainesville, FL 32610
352-265-8932
https://ufhealth.org/uf-health-shands-burn-center

University of Miami Jackson Memorial Burn Center
1611 NW 12th Avenue
Miami, FL 33136
305-585-2876
https://burn.jacksonhealth.org/

Tampa Bay Regional Burn Center
1 Tampa General Circle
Tampa, FL 33606
813-844-7141
https://www.tgh.org/services/burn

Georgia
Grady Memorial Hospital Burn Center
80 Jesse Hill Jr. Drive, SE
Atlanta, GA 30303
404-616-1000
https://www.gradyhealth.org/care-treatment/burn-center/

Joseph M. Still Burn Center
3675 J Dewey Gray Circle
Augusta, GA 30909
706-863-9595
https://doctors-hospital.net/service/about-the-burn-center

Illinois
University of Chicago Burn Center
5841 S. Maryland Avenue, South
Chicago, IL 60637
773-702-1000
https://www.uchicagomedicine.org/conditions-services/burn-center

Loyola Medicine Burn Center
2160 S 1st Avenue
Maywood, IL 60153
773-702-1000
https://loyolamedicine.org/burn-center

Indiana
Indiana University Riley Pediatric Burn Clinic
702 Riley Hospital Drive
Indianapolis, IN 46202
317-948-0345
https://www.rileychildrens.org/departments/burn-program

Eskenazi Adult Burn Center
720 Eskenazi Avenue
Indianapolis, IN 46202
317-880-0000
https://www.eskenazihealth.edu/health-services/burn-center

Iowa
University of Iowa Burn Center
200 Hawkins Drive
Iowa City, IA 52242
319-356-2496
https://uihc.org/burn-treatment-center

Kansas
Burnett Burn Center at University of Kansas Hospital
4000 Cambridge Street
Kansas City, KS 66160
913-588-5000
https://www.kansashealthsystem.com/care/specialties/burn-and-wound-care/inpatient-care

Louisiana
Baton Rouge General Regional Burn Center
8585 Picardy Avenue
Baton Rouge, LA 70809
225-387-7717
https://www.brgeneral.org/medical-services/burn/

Maryland
Johns Hopkins Adult Burn Center
4940 Eastern Avenue
Baltimore, MD 21224
410-550-0886
https://www.hopkinsmedicine.org/burn/

Michigan
University of Michigan-Trauma Burn Center
1500 E. Medical Center Drive
Ann Arbor, MI 48109
734-936-9665
https://traumaburn.org/

Children's Hospital of Michigan Pediatric Burn Center
3901 Beaubien Street
Detroit, MI 48201
313-745-5437
https://www.childrensdmc.org/services/burn-center

Detroit Medical Burn Center
4201 St Antoine
Detroit, MI 48201
313-745-3449
https://www.childrensdmc.org/services/burn-center

Massachusetts
Brigham and Women's Hospital Burn Center
75 Francis Street
Boston, MA 02115
617-732-8903
https://www.brighamandwomens.org/surgery/trauma-and-burn-center/burn-center

Shriner's Hospital for Children Boston Bun Center
51 Blossom Street
Boston, MA 02114
617-722-3000
https://www.shrinershospitalsforchildren.org/boston/burn-care

Massachusetts General Hospital-Sumner Redstone Burn Center
55 Fruit Street, GRB 1300
Boston, MA 02114
617-726-3712
https://www.massgeneral.org/burns

Minnesota
Hennepin County Burn Center
716 S 7th Street, Level 4
Minneapolis, MN 55415
612-873-2912
https://www.hennepinhealthcare.org/specialty/burn-center/

Regions Hospital Burn Center
40 Jackson Street
St Paul, MN 55101
800-922-2876
https://www.healthpartners.com/hospitals/regions/specialties/burn-center/

Missouri
Mercy Burn Center St. Louis
615 S New Ballas Road
St. Louis, MO 63141
314-251-6055
https://www.mercy.net/practice/mercy-burn-center-st-louis/

Nebraska
St. Elizabeth Regional Medical Adult Burn Center
555 S 70th Street
Lincoln, NE 68510
402-219-8000
https://www.chihealth.com/st-elizabeth/services/burn-and-wound-care.html

Nevada
UMC Lions Burns Center
1800 W Charleston Blvd
Las Vegas, NV 89102
702-383-2000
https://www.umcsn.com/Medical-Services-at-UMCSN/Lions-Wound-and-Burn-Care-Center-Index.aspx?intMenuID=132&intPageID=182

New Jersey
St. Barnabas Burn Center
94 Old Short Hills Road
Livingston, NJ 07039
973-322-5920
https://www.rwjbh.org/saint-barnabas-medical-center/treatment-care/the-burn-center/

New York
Weill Cornell Medicine-Randolph Hearst Burn Center
525 East 68th St., L-7
New York, NY 10065
646-962-2580
https://weillcornell.org/burn-center

Kessler Burn & Trauma Center
601 Elmwood Avenue
Rochester, NY 14642
585-275-2876
https://www.urmc.rochester.edu/burn-trauma/burn-center.aspx

North Carolina
North Carolina Jaycee Burn Center
101 Manning Drive # 7600
Chapel Hill, NC 27514
984-974-0150
https://www.med.unc.edu/surgery/burn/

Wake Forest Baptist Health Burn Center
Medical Center Blvd., Janeway Tower
Winston-Salem, NC 27157
336-716-3813
https://www.wakehealth.edu/Specialty/b/Burn-Center

Ohio
Akron Children's Hospital Burn Center
214 W Bowery Street, Level 3
Akron, OH 44308
330-543-8224
https://www.akronchildrens.org/locations/Burn-Center.html

Shriner's Hospital for Children-Pediatric Burn Center
3229 Burnet Avenue
Cincinnati, OH45229
855-206-2096
https://www.shrinershospitalsforchildren.org/cincinnati/burn-care

MetroHealth Burn Care Center
2500 MetroHealth Drive
Cleveland, OH 44109
216-778-2876
https://www.metrohealth.org/burn-care-center

Nationwide Children's Hospital Burn Clinic
555 South 18th Street, Suite 6F
Columbus, OH 43205
614-722-3910
https://www.nationwidechildrens.org/specialties/burn-program

Ohio State University Hospital Adult Burn Center
181 Taylor Avenue
Columbus, OH 43203
614-293-2876
https://wexnermedical.osu.edu/burn-care

Oregon
Legacy Oregon Burn Center
3001 N Gantenbein Avenue
Portland, OR 97227
503-413-2000
*https://www.legacyhealth.org/services-and-resources/services/adult/
burn-care.aspx*

Pennsylvania
Lehigh Valley Hospital Burn Center
Cedar Crest & I-78, PO Box 689, Third Floor Kasych
Allentown, PA 18105
610-402-8355
https://www.lvhn.org/locations/burn-recovery-center

Temple University Hospital Adult Burn Center
3401 N. Broad Street, Boyer Pavilion, 6th Floor
Philadelphia, PA 19140
800-TEMPLE-MED
https://www.templehealth.org/services/burn

West Penn Burn Center
4800 Friendship Avenue
Pittsburgh, PA 15224
800-TEMPLE-MED
https://www.ahn.org/services/burn-center

UPMC Mercy Burn Center
1400 Locust Street
Pittsburgh, PA 15219
412-232-7786
*https://www.upmc.com/locations/hospitals/mercy/services/
burn-center*

Nathan Speare Regional Burn Treatment Center
1 Medical Center Blvd.
Chester, PA 19013
610-447-2800
*https://www.crozerhealth.org/locations/practices/t/the-nathan-speare-
regional-burn-treatment-center/*

Rhode Island
Rhode Island Burn Center
593 Eddy Street
Providence, RI 02903
401-444-5471
https://www.lifespan.org/centers-services/rhode-island-burn-center

Tennessee
The University of Tennessee-Firefighters Regional Burn Center
877 Jefferson Avenue
Memphis, TN 38103
901-545-7100
https://www.regionalonehealth.org/main-campus/regional-medical-center/firefighters-burn-center/

Texas
Parkland Memorial Hospital Regional Burn Center
5200 Harry Hines Blvd.
Dallas, TX 75235
214-590-0168
https://www.regionalonehealth.org/main-campus/regional-medical-center/firefighters-burn-center/

US Army Institute of Surgical Research Adult Burn Center
3698 Chambers Road
San Antonio, TX 78234
210-916-3301
https://usaisr.amedd.army.mil/12_burncenter.html

Shriners Hospital for Children-Galveston Burn Center
815 Market Street
Galveston, TX 77550
409-770-6600
https://www.shrinershospitalsforchildren.org/galveston/burn-care

University of Texas Medical Branch-Blocker Burn Unit-Galveston
712 Texas Avenue, 8th Floor
Galveston, TX 77555
409-772-2023
https://www.utmbhealth.com/services/blocker-burn-unit/level-1-burn-center

Memorial Hermann John S. Dunn Burn Center
6411 Fannin, Jones Pavilion, 8th Floor
Houston, TX 77030
713-704-2500
https://trauma.memorialhermann.org/services/burn-treatment-houston/

University Medical Center Harnar Burn Center
6411 Fannin, Jones Pavilion, 8th Floor
Houston, TX 77030
713-704-2500
https://www.umchealthsystem.com/medical-services/emergent-care/services-programs/burn-care

Utah
University of Utah Hospital Burn Center
50 N Medical Drive #4
Salt Lake City, UT 84132
801-581-2700
https://healthcare.utah.edu/the-scope/shows.php?shows=0_pnhg449z

Virginia
VCU Health Evans-Haynes Burn Center
1213 E Clay Street
Richmond, VA 23219
804-828-3060
https://www.vcuhealth.org/services/evans-haynes-burn-center

Washington
UW Medicine Regional Burn Center
325 9th Avenue
Seattle, WA 98104
206-744-5735
https://www.uwmedicine.org/locations/regional-burn-center

UW Medicine Regional Burn Center
325 9th Avenue
Seattle, WA 98104
206-744-5735
https://www.uwmedicine.org/locations/regional-burn-center

Wisconsin
UW Health Burn and Wound Clinic
600 Highland Avenue
Madison, WI 53792
608-263-7502
https://www.uwhealth.org/burn-center/burn-and-wound-center/
29458

C) Burn Camps

Burn Camps serve a sensational function in building confidence and self-esteem. Most are designed for children and teens. Don't hesitate to reach out to a camp near you should this type of helpful and fun destination be appropriate for you.

Arizona
Camp Courage
1432 N. 7th Street
Phoenix, AZ 85006
(602) 230-2041

Arkansas
Camp Sunshine
2000 Aldersgate Road
Little Rock, AR 72205
501-364-2195

California
Champ Camp
50 N Hill Avenue #305
Pasadena, CA 91106
415-495-7223

AARBF Camp
350 S. Figueroa Street #395
Los Angeles, CA 90071
818-848-0223

Children's Burn Foundation Burn Camp
818-907-2822

Shriner's Hospital
800-237-5055

Firefighters Kids Camp
3101 Stockton Blvd.
Sacramento, CA 95820
916-739-8525

Camp Beyond the Scars
8825 Aero Drive, Suite 200
San Diego, CA 92123
858-541-2277

Colorado
Children's Hospital Colorado Burn Camps Program
Denver, CO
720-777-6604

Shriner's Hospital
800-237-5055

Cheley Children's Hospital Burn Camp
PO Box 1170
Estes Park, CO 80517
970-586-4244

Delaware
Burn Camp Program at the Delaware Burn Foundation
P.O. Box 682
Dover, DE 19903

District of Columbia, Washington
IAFF International Burn Camp
1750 New York Avenue, NW #300
Washington, DC 20006
202-737-8484

Georgia
Camp Oo-U-La
2575 Chantilly Drive
Atlanta, GA 30324
404-320-6223

Camp Strong Heart
1446 Harper Street
Augusta, GA 30912
706-721-1658

Illinois
Camp "I Am Me"
426 W. Northwest Highway
Mount Prospect, IL 60056
847-390-0911

Indiana
Hoosier Burn Camp
PO Box 233
Battle Ground, IN 47920
765-242-9501

Iowa
Camp Courageous
12007 190th Street
Monticello, IA 52310
319-465-5916

Maine
Fire & Ice Burn Survivors Camp
380 Congress Street
Portland, ME 04103
207-329-1276

Maryland
Mid-Atlantic Burn Camp
540 Harris Farm Lane
Clarksville, MD 21029

North Carolina
Victory Junction Gang Camp
4500 Adam's Way
Randleman, NC 27317
336-498-9055

Pennsylvania
Camp Susquehana
236 N. 17th Street
Allentown, PA 18104
610-969-3934

Tennessee
Camp Phoenix
7109 Singer Drive
Fairview, TN 37062
615-405-0438

Camp Hope
1211 21st Avenue, S.
Nashville, TN 30232
615-349-5645

Texas
Camp Aranzazu
5420 Loop 1781
Rockport, TX 78382
361-727-0800

Camp Flame Catcher
P.O. Box 255
Alpine, TX 79831
432-837-0256

Shriner's Hospital
800-237-5055

Utah
University of Utah Health Care Burn Camp Programs
50 North Medical Drive
Salt Lake City, UT 84132
801-585-2847

Virginia
Central Virginia Burn Camp
1960 Candlewyck Drive
Charlottesville, VA 22901
434-263-6566

Washington
Camp Burton
P.O. Box 806
Vashon, WA 98070
206-463-2512

Camp Phoenix
409 Wood Place
Everett, WA 98203
425-783-0560

D) Products: Pressure Garments for Wounds and Scars and Hair Products

Pressure Garments
Bio Concepts, Inc.
2424 E. University Drive
Phoenix, AZ 85034
800-421-5647
https://www.bio-con.com/

Derm Associates
10313 Georgia Avenue #309
Silver Spring, MD 20902
301-215-2890
https://www.usdermatologypartners.com/locations/maryland/silver-spring/silver-spring/

Medical Z
10625 Richmond Avenue #180
Houston, TX 77042
800-368-7478
https://www.medicalz.com/en/categorie-detail/2-custom-burn-garments

Gottfried Medical, Inc.
2920 Centennial Road
Toledo, OH 43617
800-537-1968
https://www.gottfriedmedical.com/conditions-treated/burns_surgical-complications/burns_surgical-complications.php

Luna Medical
1057 W. Grand Avenue #1
Chicago, IL 60642
800-380-4339
https://www.lunamedical.com/

BSN Medical
5825 Carnegie Blvd.
Charlotte, NC 28209
800-552-1157
https://www.bsnmedical.us/products/wound-care-vascular/category-product-search/compression-therapy/lymphedema-garments.html

Jobskin
5030 Advantage Drive #101
Toledo, OH 43612
800-207-1074
http://www.jobskingarments.com/

Active Life
1577 E Chevy Chase #210
Glendale, CA 91206
818-495-4610
https://www.4activelife.com/compression-solutions.html

D&J Compression
7600 Osler Drive # 210
Towson, MD 21204
844-365-7237
https://dandjcompression.com/

Ojmedtech
200 Carlton Avenue
East Islip, NY 11720
888-414-9737
https://www.ojmedtech.com/compression-garments/burn-garments/

Hope4Healing
2300 Computer Avenue #I-50
Willow Grove, PA 19090
215-659-4673
https://www.hope4healinginc.com/

Products for Hair Loss
Inside Out Foundation
5000 Van Nuys Boulevard #450
Sherman Oaks, CA 91403
(818) 907-2822
https://www.charitynavigator.org/

In early 2012, Co-Founders and Directors of The Inside Out Foundation (IOF), Adair Murillo and Karla Morgan, were invited to a Du (wig) party: The Du Company makes high quality synthetic wigs that are stylish, come in many lengths and colors, and are engineered to be cooler than other brands. Since Adair had worn wigs for quite some time for both fashion and convenience, this was a great opportunity for her. Shortly thereafter, Karla persuaded Adair to purchase a retail wig inventory for clients at her boutique and spa. Sharing the business opportunity with Alexis was an organic next step. While the idea was appealing to her, Alexis wanted to specifically work with need-based clients suffering from hair loss. Based on this model, Karla and Alexis networked with a local oncology nurse who runs a cancer support group. Upon presenting the Du's to the patients and their families, something special happened. The response was overwhelming (the crying kind). Simply seeing how they looked with a new, full set of hair touched them, and anyone could clearly see the joy they received from the inside, out. This was a pivotal moment for the IOF as it was a sign to move forward with our non-profit concept.

Hair Club for Kids
7900 Westpark Drive #T-100,
McLean, VA 22102
888-888-8986
https://www.hairclub.com/about-hair-club/hair-club-kids/

Hair Club for Kids program was established in 1992 to help every child a worry-free childhood with a full head of hair. They provide non-surgical hair replacement services, completely free of charge to eligible children. Their goal is to make sure every child gets the opportunity to do all the things children love to do without any restrictions due to their hair loss.

Wigs for Kids
24231 Center Ridge Rd.
Westlake, OH 44145
440-333-4433
https://www.wigsforkids.org/

Jeffrey Paul was a successful hairdresser with a thriving business. But one day, his 15-year-old niece walked into his salon, crying. She tearfully begged him to stop her hair from falling out. His immediate thoughts were that it was not serious. But when he saw the look in her father's eyes, he knew it was something more. It turned out that she had just been diagnosed with leukemia. Although chemotherapy would help save her life, it would also leave her with no hair. "I promised her that she would have hair," Paul says. "And when you make a promise to a kid, you keep it."

Hair We Share
4 Expressway Plaza, Suite LL14
Roslyn Heights, NY 11577
516-484-8483
care@hairweshare.org
https://www.wigsforkids.org/

Hair We Share was formed in 2014 and is supported by over 40 years of experience in custom design for wigs and hair pieces. We are extremely proud to say that Hair We Share is rapidly making a mark in the medical related hair loss communities, improving lives and restoring the confidence of men, women & children throughout the USA.

Hair loss is a life changing experience. Their goal is to make a positive difference in the lives of those suffering hair loss due to medical conditions. Hair We Share relies solely on donations, in the form of real-hair ponytails and monetary contributions. With these donations they provide quality hair solutions at no cost to many men, women and children throughout the USA. Hair We Share is committed to changing lives.

Hair Dreams by Christal
514 Texas Parkway, Suite A
Missouri City, TX 77489
281-499-9737
info@hairdreamsbychristal.org
https://www.hairdreamsbychristal.org/

In 2008 Hair Dreams by Christa was started with the goal to provide non-surgical hair replacement systems to underprivileged women and children who suffer from extreme long or short-term hair loss. They aim to restore people's self-esteem and rebuild their confidence by enhancing their outward appearance. Their motto is "You can be sick, but you don't have to look sick. You can have hair loss, and no one has to know it." Hair loss reaches across all social, racial and economic spectrums. It does not pick and choose who it will affect.

CHAPTER 7

An Inspiring Survivor Story

Resilience is often difficult, but astounding. Burn survivors are among the most resilient people I know. Here is a letter from a burn survivor.

It is my hope that all who undergo traumatic events come to this young woman's view of the world.

As a burn injury survivor, the scars left behind have become a part of who I am. At first, I was devastated by the sight of my body covered in scars. I felt as though I was no longer the same person I once was. But as time passed, I realized that these scars do not define me. They are a reminder of the strength and resilience that I possess.

The journey to acceptance has not been an easy one. I have struggled with the stares and comments from strangers who are unable to understand what I have been through. But I have also been blessed with the support and love of those who have stood by me through the darkest moments.

I have learned that the value of a person is not measured by their physical appearance, but by their character and inner strength. My scars are a testament to my endurance and my determination to overcome the challenges that life throws my way.

While my scars may never fade, they have taught me to embrace my imperfections and to be proud of the person I have become. I am grateful for the lessons that my journey has taught me, and I am confident that I will continue to thrive, scars and all.

CHAPTER 8

For Caregivers—Compassion Fatigue

A burn injury and its subsequent treatment are among the most painful experiences a person can encounter. For the burn victims, certainly in the early stages after the injury, the need to survive overshadows their emotional needs. For the burn victim's caregiver however, the gamut of emotions, the concerns about the victim, and the increasing understanding of the enormity of the care that will be needed for the foreseeable future can be completely overwhelming. While patients undergo various stages of adjustment and face emotional challenges that parallel the stage of physical recovery, caregivers often have no such stages, as the concern and the care needed continues.

Many people assume that when a burn patient goes home from the hospital the worst part of the recovery is over and soon life will return to "normal." In fact, most patients say that the hardest time and the "worst part" for them is when they first go home from the hospital because they don't have as much help and support as they did while in the hospital. Adult patients often cannot drive after returning home from the hospital. Almost all burn patients are required to make multiple visits back to the hospital or to an outpatient clinic for physical therapy and check-up visits. Moreover, it is usually is a lengthy period before the patient will have the energy or the mobility to do everyday chores for themselves, and it is hard for most burn survivors to ask others for help.

For children patients, their world is markedly different, and depending upon their age, their handling of their injuries will be understood, or not, and it is thus up to the caregivers, typically the parents, to be their true guardians, their protectors, their counselors. Caring for a child is certainly rewarding in "normal" situations, but also challenging. When the child is a burn victim, all measure of added responsibility and stress attaches.

Family members or friends try to make sure their loved ones' needs are met every day. Caregivers will drive to appointments, shop for groceries, prepare meals, pick up prescriptions, assist with bathing and grooming—they do it all. Unfortunately, more often than not, caregivers burn the candle at both ends.

Caregivers' issues are a real "thing." It is called compassion fatigue.

In a 2018 study, *Parental Adjustment following Pediatric Burn Injury*, conducted by Dr. Laura Hawkins, Psychologist, School of Psychology, University of Liverpool, and others:

"Parents showed high levels of psychological distress. Namely, 32.8% of mothers and 40% of fathers met clinical criteria of Post-Traumatic Stress Syndrome (PTSS), while a quarter of mothers and fathers reported symptoms indicative of moderate to severe anxiety and depression."

What is Compassion Fatigue?

Compassion fatigue occurs when caregivers become stressed from caring for others and can be thought of as extreme burnout. It doesn't just happen overnight. As days, weeks and months (in some cases years) march on with mounting responsibilities, caregivers become overwhelmed physically, emotionally, spiritually and socially. The following are some signs and symptoms associated with compassion fatigue:

- You are irritable
- You find you are ability to function is decreasing
- You are pulling back from normal activities
- You are cancelling plans
- You have increasing aches and pains
- You are feeling bored and apathetic
- You are suffering from fatigue, and you are feeling tired and worn out
- You are forgetting things and having memory problems
- You feel depressed and excessively anxious
- You have emotional outbursts, e.g., crying, anger, etc.
- You are having problems sleeping
- You overreact to trivialities and are impatient with your loved one
- You are developing health issues
- You feel like you cannot relax
- You have let yourself and your needs go

- You are not interested, or not as interested, in intimate relations with a partner

Not only does dealing with high levels of stress affect your ability to provide care, it also puts your own health and well-being at risk. Lack of sleep, not eating right, trying to do too much, stressing about things you cannot change, and not seeking out emotional support for yourself while dealing with the stresses of caring for someone <u>will</u> take its toll on you.

Once you burn out, caregiving is no longer a healthy option for either you or the person you're caring for. It's important to watch for the warning signs of caregiver burnout and take action right away when you recognize the problem. Below are some of the signs that your stress levels are reaching burnout level:

It is important to tend to your own physical needs (sleep, rest, nutrition, exercise, etc.) and take time off. Don't be afraid or ashamed to ask trusted family or friends for help.

Is it Possible to Combat?

The first step in combatting compassion fatigue is to recognize and be aware that it is present. If you are a caregiver and the above discussion rings true in your life, you might consider getting professional help (there is nothing wrong with seeking such help and it is a sign of intelligence and strength to do so), and you should absolutely let others know how you are doing, and ask for their help. The following are some suggestions on how to make this happen:

Start with a half-day off. If a full day off from caregiving isn't possible, start with a half day. But it shouldn't be a one-and-done happening. Try to schedule half-days off on a regular basis to avoid compassion fatigue.

Phone a family member or friend. Ask for assistance from another family member who can pitch in and help care for your loved one for the day. Even better would be to set up a rotating schedule for help.

Tap into available community resources. A quick search in the Internet can provide many organizations that are ready to help you.

Regain balance. Setting unrealistic goals for yourself will increase your stress. Understand when your expectations are too high. You will often have countless tasks given to you by many people. To get back on track, set limits and be prepared to say "no" when it is necessary.

Take time for yourself. When things go wrong, it is common to feel you can't do one more thing, but it isn't a sign of failure or weakness. Stop and take care of yourself. It is not being selfish to take some time for yourself. Caregivers cannot help others if they are not balanced.

Express yourself. You can avoid compassion fatigue by being mindful of feelings inside and out. Feelings can be expressed verbally by talking with someone, or journaling can be beneficial when writing about the entire experience.

Take a deep cleansing breath or two. Deep breathing exercises can help decrease stress and allow time to regroup.

Helping Children Cope with a Burn Injury

Going through a traumatic event such as a burn accident and sustaining major injuries can cause significant feelings of loss and grief amongst both adult and child survivors. Children may go through the grieving process and demonstrate many changes in behavior during their recuperation. In addition to using individual and family counseling and psychological therapies, there are many other strategies parents can use when helping children cope with a burn injury.

Family-centered care is based on the belief that the family is a child's primary source of strength and support. Healthcare professionals are the experts on health and disease. Parents are the experts on their children, and they can offer essential information to enhance their child's health care. A successful partnership between healthcare providers and families is based on mutual trust, respect and responsibility. **Montreal Children's Patient and Family Centered Care Policy**

Family members and parents then are an integral part of the team, and therefore should accompany the child during all procedures. The presence of parents will reassure and comfort the child, and it will allow the parents to see the evolution of the healing process.

Some of the losses child burn survivors may have to face include (as repeated here and first mentioned in the Chapter "Special Considerations For Children"):

- The loss of their prior appearance
- The loss of their pre-injury lifestyle and recreational activities
- The loss of a limb or limited mobility and range of motion
- The loss of certain dreams and hopes for their future
- The loss of other loved ones or pets in the accident that caused their injuries

- The loss of their home and possessions
- The loss of friends and family relationships

Consider these tips for helping your child cope with loss but remember that these tips may not be appropriate for children of all ages. Work with professional to find age-appropriate options.

Remember Mr. or Ms. Caregiver: You must take care of yourself to then be able to take care of others. They tell you when you get seated on the airplane that "in the event of an incident, put your mask on first, and then on your child." It is a labor of love to care for someone else. Remember yourself when you are trying to meet the needs of your loved one.

In connection with getting help to care for your child, please consider "burn camps."

Burn Camps for Children—I repeat this here from the chapter on Children, because sending a child to camp is beneficial for both the child and the parents

The International Association of Burn Camps (IABC) provides a network for the mutual benefit of local and regional organizations that serve the burn community. These camps support the physical, social, and psychological needs of children and teenage burn survivors and their families. For more information, log on to:

http://www.iaburncamps.org/membership/member-camps/

CHAPTER 9

For Attorneys—Know Your Client and Your Theory

This chapter is being written for novice attorneys, and for others who have not experienced the difficult but rewarding representation involving a burn survivor, or the family of someone who died because of burns.

For a novice attorney, there is only one piece of advice here: associate with an attorney experienced in complex cases, most appropriately, one familiar with and experience in handling product liability cases.

The number one thing I want to share is that handling a burn injury case successfully involves, perhaps more than any other type of injury case, telling your client's story.

For those attorneys experienced in complex cases, but who have not handled a burn injury case, understand that the single distinctive difference between a burn injury case and others is that the path to recovery for a burn victim is never the same as any other. Every burn injury survivor will have a different path to both physical and psychological recovery, and as counsel, you must be prepared to both follow and guide, and understand the pacing and the progress. These injuries can span years before any semblance of recovery is appreciated. This understanding of your client's ever evolving status then underlies all you will do in working with the client.

Then, like other complex cases, the first real "action" on your part is gathering "causation" facts. This is the investigation stage. The beginning of any investigation, of course, is a thorough conversation with the client and any others who might have direct knowledge of the event. It involves having details conversations with all "immediate" people around the event, from a "witness" perspective and from a knowledge perspective—any who know anything about the cause of the event, the status of the equipment, or the apparatus, and the conditions. Getting an expert witness involved in the early stages of the investigation is important as their guidance can be invaluable in many ways.

Continuing investigation involves identifying other individuals who have knowledge of the events and who can provide information about how the event occurred or who might offer thoughts on why it occurred.

At some point, you must determine your theory or theories of liability, and this of course will be based in large part upon your investigation. You understand you can make claims based on negligence, strict liability, breach of warranty or fraud.

Negligence

In a case based on negligence, as you know, the plaintiff must typically prove that:

- the defendant owed the plaintiff a duty of reasonable care under the circumstances (i.e. by making or selling a product, the manufacturer or seller had a legal obligation to make sure that product was free from dangerous defects and unreasonable or hidden risks)
- the defendant's actions (putting a dangerous product into the marketplace) breached the duty owed to the plaintiff, and
- the plaintiff actually suffered some kind of injury (*"damages"*) as a result of the defendant's actions.

Breach of Warranty

In a breach of warranty case, the plaintiff must show that:

- an express or implied warranty applied to the product, and
- the product did not meet the terms of the warranty

Fraud

For a "fraud" legal theory you must show that:

- the defendant made certain representations about the product
- those representations were not true
- the defendant knew the representations were not true (or were unlikely to be true)

- the defendant made the representations so that the plaintiff would buy the product

- your client was justified in relying on the defendant's representations, and

- your client was damaged in some way because of the defendant's false representations.

If the facts of the case fit a fraud theory, a defendant may be ordered to pay punitive damages based on its intentional deception. In those somewhat rarer product liability cases that do involve fraud, the punitive damages award can end up being quite high, since this kind of award is typically set relative to a defendant's assets.

Strict Liability

Strict liability cases are different from other personal injury cases. In strict product cases, there is no need to prove negligence. The only evidence needed is proof of injury and proof of the product's defect to meet strict liability standards.

Once the injury is verified and the defect established, you have met their burden of proof. Then it's up to the manufacturer to prove the product wasn't defective.

Strict Liability Cases: Categories of Defects

A manufacturer may be found liable for injuries caused by one or more categories of product defects.

Design defects are mistakes or inherent flaws in a product. In most cases, the flaws are built into the product when it's manufactured, but flaws can also occur during design modifications.

Manufacturing defects can occur even if the product's design was not faulty. A product can be inherently flawless in its design, but by the time it comes off the assembly line, it can be defective.

Marketing defects ("Failure to Warn") happen when the manufacturer doesn't provide the user with enough information to use the product safely or misstates a product's benefits.

In other words, on behalf of your client, you could seek compensation from any party which helped bring the defective product to market, including:

A company who made parts for the defective product;

The company who installed or assembled the product;

The store that sold the product.

Defenses to Strict Liability

Strict liability is not automatic. Some types of products are inherently dangerous, such as gasoline, table saws, carving knives, and other types of products that would not work for their intended purpose if they were made "harmless." However, the manufacturer must provide ample warning of the danger to consumers.

Manufacturers may escape liability if they can prove one or more of the following:

The design, manufacture, and marketing of the product was flawless

The victim's misuse or abuse of the product was responsible for their injuries

The victim was aware of the defect and its danger and used the product anyway

The victim ignored the warning label or instructions

If a manufacturer can prove any of the above circumstances, strict liability will not be automatic. Instead, the burden of proof will shift back to your client, who then has to disprove the manufacturer's defenses.

Strict Liability Is Typically the Main Theory

For two main reasons, strict product liability will likely be the main focus of your burn injury case for your client. It is the assertion that represents the biggest threat to a defendant manufacturer or seller.

This is clearer when we understand that in order to make a successful case based on a negligence or fraud theory, the plaintiff needs to prove a number of additional elements. The plaintiff's "burden of proof" is easier to meet in a strict liability case.

Second, strict liability allows a plaintiff to recover the full range of damages available in a typical *personal injury case* (including compensation for *«pain and suffering.»* In contrast, compensation in a breach of warranty case can often be limited to concrete economic damages (e.g. damage to property, medical bills, etc.), and usually excludes "pain and suffering" damages.

Case Progress

As noted, building a burn injury case begins with your investigation. You start, obviously, by hearing your client's story. Then you must gather extensive additional information, that will certainly include the following, and potentially more:

- Your client's testimony
- The defective product itself
- Photos of the defective product
- Photos and medical documentation of injuries
- Accident reconstruction from an expert witness
- Statements of third-party witnesses
- Documentation of financial losses and damages
- Expert testimony about the severity and duration of injuries
- Expert testimony about the link between the product defect and injuries

The defective product in your case may be the only defective product of its kind, or it may be one of many defective products. Your will research to see if there are other incidents like that may be helpful to prove your case.

The early days following an accident can often be critical in setting the stage for a successful product liability action. The product or "thing" that injures a client must be secured, or at the very least thoroughly examined, as soon as possible to assure that its condition will not be changed.

If possible, the defective product should be locked in a facility that you control. The product that injured your client should never be disposed of unless it presents a risk of immediate harm. Major manufacturers are immediately aware of product recalls and they carefully read newspapers, so they may attempt to secure evidence to deny you the ability to pursue claims.

If the product cannot be secured immediately, put everyone on notice, including tow-truck operators, wrecking yards, and police impounds that they must take every step to preserve the product, which is evidence, and that the failure to do so will subject them to liability for allowing evidence to be destroyed. When the product is in the possession of a third party or one of the potential defendants, you might immediately file an action for a temporary restraining order and a preliminary injunction to avoid alterations to or destructive testing of the product.

You will want to obtain the complete history of the product and seek to determine the date of the original sale, identity of the dealer, distributor, subsequent purchasers, lessees and users. It is important to locate the instruction booklet, assembly booklet, warranties and all other written material that accompanied the new product at the time of the original sale and distribution. You need to determine if the product was modified or otherwise changed after it left the possession of the manufacturer and distributor and, if so, the identity of the persons or entities that made the modification, and the dates involved.

More on Experts

A successful liability case will usually require the assistance and testimony of an expert. Typical types of experts retained are engineers, safety experts, and medical professionals. Finding a qualified expert early in the litigation process is usually the major factor in successfully proving your case.

Expert engineering testimony is often crucial to proving that a design or manufacturing defect in a product caused the plaintiff's injuries. In addition to utilizing engineering testimony, you might rely on the testimony of psychologists or experts specializing in the field of human factors. This is because sometimes, a strict engineering approach fails to consider that a product must be designed not only to work, but also so that people can safely use it. A biomechanical analysis can reveal a hidden danger for the unwary user or a practical way to prevent injuries, based on an understanding of human tendencies and behaviors.

In appropriate cases, expert testing, either destructive or nondestructive, of the product at issue may be necessary to determine whether there is evidence that the product failed or could fail in the manner detailed by your client and witnesses.

The Discovery Process

The discovery process may include requesting records of designs or information about the manufacturing process. It may involve requiring employees to testify under oath about their products or production of the specific product in question. Using the discovery process to gather records can be helpful to prove how the product is defective. When used effectively, discovery can narrow the issues in dispute and make your products liability case stronger.

Extensive discovery should be conducted to determine if the Defendants have been sued before. A potential punitive damages claim is possible if you can show repeated knowledge of a problem and a failure to resolve it.

Conclusion

This is not about telling you how to try a case my dear colleague; I am confident you know how to do that. I hope the introductory information here, however, was helpful, and once again, I repeat that the strength of this case, after everything considered, is more about your client than in almost any other type of injury claim. Get your client's story and make sure you tell it.

CHAPTER 10

FAQ's and SAQ's—Frequently Asked and Should Ask Questions

Many of my clients ask me, and appropriately, many of these questions. In fact, many people have these questions in mind after they have been injured.

A) FAQ's

Do I Have a Case?

If you have been injured, it is 100% ALWAYS advisable to speak to an attorney. If you do not have a case, so be it—but not investigating if you have a case, particularly if you do, would be a colossal mistake.

While in "simple" cases such as a "rear-end" automobile accident, the answer to "do I have a case" is very easy. In more complex cases, such as burn injury cases, determining if you have a case can be difficult to answer right away, and will come usually after a preliminary investigation, but sometimes, not until a bit more thorough investigation. But generally, your lawyer can determine if you should move forward with a lawsuit after hearing the details and outlining the strengths and weaknesses of your case.

What is My Case Worth?

We will find out. We can't possibly know now. We have to wait until we have all of the facts, and learn how bad your injury is, and if it is permanent, or disabling. We must know how much time you missed from work and the amount of money you lost, the amount of your medical bills, and much, much more.

We don't know the score of the baseball game in the first inning. But we will find out what the score is when the game is over. Your case evaluation begins when the medical treatment is over.

How Long Will the Process Take?

It depends. Don't you hate that answer? I do, too. But the truth is that it can take months or years to come to a conclusion in your case. Many factors will play into this, such as whether you're looking at a settlement or a court case, the amount of monetary compensation you're seeking or that is appropriate, the complexity of your case, and whether extensive investigations need to take place. If a case cannot be settled "out of court" There are filing deadlines, proceedings, hearings, investigations, reports, and much more to go through. Your burn injury attorney can give you a ballpark timeframe but at the beginning, it can be nearly impossible to tell with certainty how long it will take from start to finish.

Do I need to hire an attorney about my burn accident?

First, please see Chapter Two of this book—Why You Should Consult An Attorney.

Next, if the answer to the above question is not clear yet, let me be emphatic—YES YES YES—ALWAYS hire an attorney if you have suffered a burn injury.

You are not legally trained. You do not have the knowledge or ability to know what to do or how to do it.

You present no "threat" to the insurance company. They LOVE when people try to settle cases by themselves, because:

1. They will have to pay less as the injured person does not know the value of their case;
2. They will have to pay less because the injured person does not know how to document their case;
3. They will have to pay less because the injured person does not know how to file a lawsuit, conduct the pre-trial process, or properly "try" the case in front of a jury;
4. They will have to pay less because the injured person will be going up against a trained, experienced and savvy attorney who represents the at-fault party.

What if I Cannot Afford a Lawyer?

Not a problem. You do not pay anything until the case is over and either a settlement or verdict in your favor is obtained. Lawyers who handle Personal injury claims work on a contingency basis. This means that rather than requiring you to pay upfront for their services, they only charge you a percentage of your settlement—and only if and when they win your case. You will not have any initial out-of-pocket expenses. In the event the attorney does not recover a settlement, you may be responsible for costs, but there is no "attorney's fee."

This arrangement postpones the payment of all your legal services until after the case has been successfully resolved, again, either through a negotiated settlement or a jury trial award.

Where Can I Find a Lawyer Who Handles Burn Injury Cases?

Aside from the obvious self-serving answer here: me, a larger answer is to investigate. See the SAQ's (should ask questions) in the next chapter.

What Types of Damages Can I Recover in a Burn Injury Case?

First, please see Chapter Two of this book—Why You Should Consult An Attorney and Components of Legal Claims.

In summary then, you may recover damages for most of your injury-related losses, both tangible losses (economic or special damages) and intangible losses (non-economic or general damages). Compensation can include current and future medical bills, lost wages, disability, scarring and disfigurement, emotional and psychological harm, and the effect of the injury on your wellbeing, family life, and career.

In some cases, you may also be entitled to recover punitive damages. These damages are provided where there is proof of a very high level of negligence. Particularly, these damages can be awarded for reckless or intentional behavior on the part of the Defendant, and in all cases, this is "extra" money for you, designed to punish the wrongdoer.

What Happens If I am Partially at Fault For Causing My Accident?

Again, please see Chapter Two of this book—Why You Should Consult An Attorney and Components of Legal Claims.

To answer this question here—there are two very distinct and different laws in the United States. Five states are "contributory negligence" law states. This means if you were even one percent at fault, you get nothing, because you contributed to your injury.

In all of the other states, the law is called "comparative negligence." This means, if you were partially at fault, whatever percentage is determined to be "your fault" is used to decrease, by the same percentage, from your recovery. Thus, in a simple example, if you are ten percent at fault and your win $100 at trial, ten percent is deducted due to your fault, and you'd then get $90.

B) SAQ's

Have You Handled Similar Cases?

Burn injury law is a "subset" of "personal injury" law. Personal injury law includes anything from motorcycle and motor vehicle accidents to dog bites and slips and falls. Handling burn injury cases is more complicated. That is the reason it is important to ask your attorney if he or she has experience with burn injury cases. You want someone with the experience and skill necessary know what to investigate, how to do so, and then to present your case properly to first insurance companies, and then if necessary, in a courtroom to a jury. Don' be afraid to ask about their experience and years in the business. It is in your best interests to hire a qualified attorney who is experienced with burn injuries.

What is Your Case Strategy?

All lawyers have a proven strategy for winning cases and reaching settlements. Some are extremely aggressive and leave nothing to chance, while others prefer to take a more laid back, methodical approach. Some want to set the wheels in motion immediately, others prefer to gather more background information, and still, others will tell you an immediate settlement is the best way to go. The strategy that best suits you will be a matter of personal opinion. Find out what their strategy is, the pros and cons, and how this strategy has worked to their advantage in the past.

Is there a Time Limit for Taking Legal Action?

Yes, each state has a distinct time limit, called the Statute of Limitations. This is an absolute time limit deadline, defining the date by-which you must file a lawsuit. Most states have a two- or three-year time limit. This means that, starting with the date the injury occurred (the date the "clock starts to run"), you have two, or three, or whatever number of years after that date, to either reach a voluntary "out of court" settlement, or you must file the lawsuit. If you do not settle or file the lawsuit within that deadline, your case is over and you get nothing. Filing your lawsuit within the time limit protects your claim. When and if a trial actually takes place is not the concern… it is the filing of the lawsuit by the deadline date. Accordingly, as investigation of the case can be more and more difficult the further out from the injury event, it is advisable to get started with an attorney as soon as possible, to maximize the preservation of evidence, witness testimony and arranging for "experts" to become involved. The sooner the "case" begins, the more likely the financial compensation result will be better.

For children, the "clock" starts to run when the child becomes an adult (age 18). Thus, for a child who is in a state where the Statute of Limitations is two years, the child's "deadline" is on that child's twentieth birthday.

Whom Can I Hold Legally Responsible for My Injuries?

Determining liability comes after a thorough and complete investigation has been conducted, so learning who is ultimately responsible (and there may be more than one responsible party) will vary from case to case. Defendants in burn injury cases may be individuals (a neighbor who started a fire that spread to your house/started a fire in your house), business (a manufacturer of a defective product), or other entities (a city or organization that caused an explosion). In many cases, it is not just a reckless or negligent action that led to the event, but a malfunctioning product or faulty equipment that caused the accident. That said, there may be multiple defendants in your case including a property owner, equipment manufacturer, machinery installer, gas company, electrical company, or others. Your attorney will help you determine the liable party in your case.

What do I do if my burn accident occurred on the job?

If you suffered a burn injury on the job, you usually cannot sue your employer. Rather, you will a claim for workers' compensation benefits, which includes payment for lost income, all medical bills and rehabilitation. However, in some cases, you may be able to sue a third party. An example might be a worker who was injured due to a boiler or heater exploding. In this instance the manufacturer of the boiler or heater might be responsible under a theory of poor product design. Moreover, a technician charged with maintenance in that example might be negligent, and a claim might then be made against the technician if the maintenance was not done, or done improperly. In this example, the injured worker would have two claims—a workers' compensation claim AND a "third party" claim.

What Can I Expect During the Legal Process?

There are numerous steps to the legal process, including filing a claim, gathering evidence, negotiating with the insurer, and going through litigation if necessary. You may encounter a challenging and lengthy legal process, but an attorney can help you navigate it.

Keep in mind that taking legal action may be worth your efforts because if your case is successful, you may secure the funds you need to cover your burn care and compensate you for other financial and emotional losses.

What Happened is Pretty Clear. Why Does my Attorney Need Hire Experts to Prove my Case?

First, because insurance companies that ultimately might have to pay these claims ALWAYS fight, and deny that their insured (the defendant) is responsible. The very nature of paying claims goes against their effort to make money by selling insurance. So, having experts who can prove what happened is essential.

Next, again, while the "facts" might be obvious, by law, you will need to prove exactly what happened, and how a negligent or intentional act directly caused your injuries, and you must identify who committed the irresponsible, reckless or negligent act. It is one thing to say, for example, the boiler exploded. It is another to prove exactly what happened and why it exploded. The law requires that "higher level" of proof. Only qualified experts can provide that proof.

Finally, experts can provide, based on their specialized field of knowledge, the exact details about what happened and why. These professional witnesses might be an engineer, a gas expert, a building expert, or an investigator. A doctor is needed as an expert witness to explain the extent of your injuries and why you need so much monetary compensation to recover from your injuries, and what will be needed to maintain your normal activities after your recovery.

Conclusion:
Choosing An Attorney to Represent You

There are many, and superb attorneys in our country. A smaller number of them have handled burn injury claims. An even smaller number of them have handled many burn injury claims.

Choose wisely, it can make a difference.

I am licensed to practice law, since 1980. I practice in Maryland and Virginia. When I have a client in another state, I associate with another highly experienced attorney, because in order to file a lawsuit and go to court in any given state, one of the attorneys must be licensed in that state. Working with other attorneys provides extra benefits to clients, as they get the benefit of having "two heads" (which are normally better than one) for "the price of one."

My Office:

Provides Care and Guidance

We provide care and guidance and help you through the devastating circumstances you find yourself in. We work to make sure that your health, your family and your loved ones can be provided for now and in the future.

Holds Wrongdoers Accountable

We investigate what happened to you, get answers, and hold wrongdoers accountable.

Works to Secure Your Future

We've won millions of dollars for my clients and dramatically improved their lives.

Never Asks for "Costs" or any Money at all, Until and Unless We Win

We work on a contingency basis, which means you never owe us anything unless we recover damages for you. My firm has the resources to get qualified expert witnesses and pay for visuals that will make your case and testimony come alive in court.

May your recovery be quick, and may your life be wonderful. Your injuries do not define you. I hope you have found value in this book. I would love to talk to you, and if you want to consider working with me, that will be my highest honor, and truly, the highest compliment.

The Law Offices of Paul A. Samakow
My personal mobile telephone: 703-472-7688